My Impossible Dream

Florence and Brother Le Roy Dockter

My Impossible Dream

You Can Do It Too

FLORENCE DOCKTER SCHERBENSKE

MILL CITY PRESS

Mill City Press, Inc.
2301 Lucien Way #415
Maitland, FL 32751
407.339.4217
www.millcitypress.net

Printed in the United States of America.

Paperback ISBN-13: 978-1-6322-1978-7
eBook ISBN-13: 978-1-6322-1977-0

TABLE OF CONTENTS

Dedication xi

Acknowledgements xiii

Preface. xv

1. Wedding, Farm Purchase. 1
The Marriage, Honeymoon – The Farm Purchase

2. Dockter Family. 11
Dockter Family, Ukraine To America
Records of Childhood Family
Grandfather Gottlieb Dockter Jr. Man Of Wisdom (Part 1)
Dear Grandma, Gottlieb Dockter Jr., Farmer, Generous
Dear Grandma, Mother Helen, Youth
Grandfather Gottlieb Dockter Jr. Man Of Wisdom (Part 2)
From Sod House To Wood House
Grandfather Gottlieb Dockter Jr., Venturia Home
Dear Grandma, Grandfather Dockter Driving Car, 1929
    Financial Crash
Ukranish Baptismal Cap
The Historic Book
Dear Grandma, Christian Dockter, Bone Setter, Chiropractor
Dear Grandma, Phillip Dockter, California
Dear Grandma, Admiration and Courage
Dear Grandma, Christine Gifted A Washing Machine

3. Helfenstein Family.. 24
  Ancestry, Maternal
  Dear Grandma, Helfenstein Family, Ship To America, Settled In
    North Dakota
  Dear Grandma, Ages Of Your Children When Your First
    Husband Died
  Dear Grandma, From Germany To Ukraine, Then To America
  Great Grandparents' Home, Yard, City Cow
  Dear Grandma, Uncle Johann Jr. Farm
  Dear Grandma, Death of Johann Helfenstein Jr.
  Dear Grandma, Lost On A Foggy Day
  Dear Grandma, Grandpa Esch — 1918 Influenza
  My Great Grandparents Helfenstein
  Dear Grandma, The Truth...You Are Loved
  Dear Grandma, Widow, Moved To Be Near Parents
  My Grandma Katie
  Dear Grandma, Rain Would Have Saved Everything
  The Orphan Train

4. John Ritter and Children................................. 38
  Dear Grandma, John Ritter, Children
  Dear Grandma, Helen and Carrie
  Dear Grandma, The Icehouse
  Our First Family Car
  Dear Grandma, I Should Have Written It Down
  Dear Grandma, Edna

5. Florence Schooling..................................... 43
  Crazy Pony Transportation
  Country School
  Male Domination and German Background
  Childhood Memories, Schooling
  Confirmation Day
  Recovering From Shame and Rejection

6. Childhood Responsibilites............................... 49
  Self-Sufficiency

Cleaning Mother's House
Scrubbing the Kitchen Floor
Dear Grandma, I Created Running Water
Annual Meat Preparation

7. **Inez** 55
The Sheep Buck Saw Me
Dear Grandma, Inez Recovers, Local Stores and Mom's Hand-
tooled Purse
The Little Town of Venturia
My Most Embarrassing Moment
My First Flower Garden
The Attic In Our Two-Room House
More Confusion, Passing On Shame
Dear Grandma, Letter One

8. **Sibling Death - Florence Pearl, Stanley Julius** 64
Florence Pearl, Stanley Julius, and Gladys
Dear Grandma, Six Months After The First Stanley Died
Dear Grandma, Memories of Stanley Julius
Mr. Baglow, Life Insurance Agent

9. **Cooking** 73
German Russia Cooking
German Russia Dough Dishes, Food Preservation
Closing-Quick Meal Stove – A Life Saved
Grandfather Dockter, Butchering and Canning a Cow
Dear Grandma, Cookstove and Mischt
My Mother-In-Law
A Pioneer Woman
Dear Grandma, Forever Yeast–"Avigar Sautz"

10. **The Chick Project** 84
"Shadows of the Past" — The Chick Project
Father Getting Chickens To Lay Eggs
The Treacherous Turn – State Highway 11 / County Road
Our Flock of Sheep

11. World War II 91
Dear Grandma, World War II

12. Beginning Travel 117
Trip to the Twin Cities

13. The Winter of 1950 120
The Winter of 1950

14. Farming 124
Electricity and Running Water
The Dugout, Cross Fencing
My Farm Business Contribution
Heavy Farm Equipment
Mystery Garden
The Shetland

15. Friendship Force 133
The Good Old Days, Travel in the Late 60's, Central America
The Friendship Force
Friendship Force in Russia 1981-82
Friendship Force – Finland, Russia – Original Notes
Friendship Force – Egypt

16. Divorce 143
Cooking In My Teenage Marriage/Silent Treatment
Dear Grandma, My Marriage Came to an End

17. Goodbye Elder 146
Goodbye, Elder Scherbenske
Thank You, Elder Scherbenske
Closure: Overcoming Childhood Stress
Beginning Experience

18. Climbing the Mountain 151
Climbing the Mountain, Self-Encounter

19. 4-H Related Activities, Jocie, Glenny 155
My Cousin, Mildred Dockter, and 4-H

Bonnie and Betty Flemmer
Tangerine, Wool Suit
Jocie's Wedding Dress 1973
Jocie – Area Woman of Fargo
Glenny's Employer's Christmas Letter To Me, 2018
Glenny's Adventures

20. Recovering from Shame 163
Closure – Shame
The Receiver of Shame

21. Lee 165
Lee

22. Health Failure 168
Health Failure 2016
Getting Back Into Society

23. Personal Development and Accomplishments 172
Florence Dockter Scherbenske–Personal Development–
    Resume 1987
Closure - My Accomplishments In Life, Self-Education, Personal
    Development
Graduation from American High School, Chicago Illinois

24. Leadership and Accomplishments. 177
Rosebud Mission Program
The Hoarder
Quilt Making / My Quilt Collection
Munsingwear Fabric

25. Closure 182
Closure–My Mother's Hard Life
My Parents Provided and Cared For Us
Rise Above Many Obstacles

26. In A Nutshell 185
In A Nutshell (Recorded in Library of Congress)

DEDICATION

I give tribute to my maternal grandmother, Katherine Helfenstein Esch Ritter, for the love and kindness she gave me when I was a child. Also, for the letters she wrote to me when I was growing up. She came as a German from Russia immigrant to America at age eight. She was married to Heinrich Esch. He died in the 1918 Influenza, and left her a widow with five children under the age of ten. She endured the hardship of that time.

I give tribute to my paternal grandfather, Gottlieb Dockter Jr., who was a man of wisdom and generosity, and was well respected in his community. He taught his six sons the industry and art of farming and livestock. He was a German from Russia immigrant. After hard work and hardships, he acquired enough property to set up each of his sons in farming. It was a benefit to my parents and to us siblings. We had the good fortune to have food and a house to live in during the dust storms and depression of the 1930's.

ACKNOWLEDGEMENTS

Thank you Karen Ciszczon.

I want to give a special thanks to Karen for searching and digging through all my cursive hand written ten notebooks and transcribing all my manuscripts into a hard copy and online. We enjoyed the many hours we spent working on the script. This would not have been possible without you.

PREFACE

You Can Do It Too!

I proved to myself that no matter how many obstacles there are in life, I could rise above them. I rose above it. You Can Do It Too!

The reason I wrote this book.

I grew up in a home never having a childhood, was not allowed to go to high school, and had a teenage marriage. I took charge of my life and lived a life of volunteer, business and hard work. I worked hard to overcome the physical and mental abuse in my childhood which continued into my adulthood.

To the reader: Never give up. You can take charge of your life. I did, and you can do it too.

WEDDING, FARM PURCHASE

The Marriage, Honeymoon – The Farm Purchase

Art Rudolph began dating me a few days after my sixteenth birthday. He came each weekend on Sunday afternoon. We met his sister, Alice, in Venturia, North Dakota, and then he took me to the movie. He drove back to his home at night.

One week before my seventeenth birthday (October), he said, "If we are going to get married, we should do it now and leave for a honeymoon out west to Oregon in November." He did not ask for my hand in marriage. I told my parents about the marriage plans and asked them to take me to Ashley and sign for parental consent. My parents were not happy and asked me if I was pregnant. I was not.

My parents lived fifty miles from the Rudolph family. The first time they met was when Matt and Sofie Rudolph came to the Dockter farm to plan the wedding. In those days, there were no paved state roads and no telephone.

The wedding was a two-week planning affair. I did not want a big wedding. My mother wanted the big wedding. She gave me $50. Art and I went to Aberdeen, South Dakota to shop for clothes. I went to Ovin and Angel and bought a white taffeta dress off the half price rack.

I did not want a satin dress (that is another story.) The dress had a sheer neckline, back boucle, and a five-foot train. The total cost was $25. The finger-tipped veil and crown were $17. Somehow, I found a pair of gold sandals, a girdle (that was too small) to hold up the stockings and a strapless bra that almost killed me. I managed to buy these items for $8. I talked my mother into buying two yards of pink wide wale corduroy with which I managed to sew a coat for the wedding.

Our wedding was planned for October 22, 1948. The night before the wedding, there was a rehearsal which turned out to be a disaster. The Pastor Rev. Krueger came to Ashley, North Dakota, from Germany four years before. He believed "...women should be silent in the church." The church was very small. He told us the service was about one hour and insisted that we have chairs to seat the bride and groom and our bridal attendants. The only thing I could think of was my dress, the boucle, and the five-foot train. I knew there was no reasoning in that man, so being the bride, I left early.

My first experience with the pastor was three years before. My parents wanted me to memorize the Heidelberg catechism in high German – which was impossible for me because I could not read high German. They thought I should do this to please Grandfather. After three weeks, I told my mother that I would not go back to the six-week confirmation class because Pastor Krueger did all the lecturing in English. My father suggested that Mother should take me to the pastor and discuss the problem. The pastor reasoned that it was a good idea to teach in English because it is the language of our country. I was the first person confirmed in English in our little Reformed church!

The rehearsal was a disaster. I slept very little that night. The pastor may not have slept much that night either. After the rehearsal, we thought he left the church. Some of the things that were said in our group were not nice about the pastor. To our surprise, he had been eavesdropping. Something happened to him. Perhaps he confided secretly to his beautiful, humble wife – everyone loved her. Or perhaps an angel spoke to him.

The next afternoon, Art and I went to Wishek to pick up the flowers. That was a disappointment because I ordered pink and white carnations and they substituted pink and white mums. Pricewise, roses were not used much in those days.

We went to the Ashley bakery to pick up the wedding cake about 4:00 p.m. – three hours before the wedding. A clerk asked us what we wanted.

"We came to get the wedding cake."

She said, "What cake?"

We said, "The Dockter/Rudolph cake."

She went to the calendar, then shouted, "Kenny, come out here."

The calendar showed an order for a three-layer cake for October 22. She was upset and excited. She assured us the cake would be ready and on the bride's table on time. Later, when the wedding party arrived for the reception in Venturia, there was a beautiful six tier cake on the table! The bakery went from a three tier to a six layer which cooled much faster in time to apply the frosting. It was more beautiful and expensive than the one we ordered!

The wedding was in the Ashley church and we invited about 300 guests. The evening of the wedding, the congregation was already seated. Pastor Krueger must have realized that he was dealing with Florence. He may have recalled the confirmation experience. He met me at the door and said he changed his mind. There would be no chairs to seat the bridal party and the sermon would be short.

The wedding went well. However, my five-foot train did not trail because the entrance and aisle were short. It fell in a pile. My uncle said it looked like an expensive broom.

The dinner reception was at the Venturia City Hall which was constructed by WPA in the late thirties and still stands. Looking at it now, it is hard to imagine 300 people standing up in an area of that size. How could they be seated and served?

After dinner and cake, all the gifts were opened so the guests could see the gift and from whom it was given. By then it was midnight. We went back to Ashley for the wedding dance. The crowd was small, and the hall was not heated and very cold. I wore my pink, wide wale corduroy coat and was lucky to have it! The only heat we had was the wine that my father, Julius Dockter, supplied and there was plenty of it.

The dance lasted until 4:00 that morning. Jakie Schlepp and his wife, Violet Wolf, so graciously invited us to be guests at their house that morning. We slept in the only bedroom they had. I do not know where they slept. They served us a nice breakfast. We went to Venturia to load all the gifts in our car and to help with some of the cleaning up. Later that afternoon, we went to the Rudolph farm which was fifty miles away. There were no phones. The only communication was by mail.

Art's father, Matt Rudolph, planned to have his farm sale two weeks after our wedding. It would be the first week in November. All the cattle and machinery were to be sold, but he would not sell the land. His wish was that his sons would continue farming it. The family farm consisted of a total of 1,600 acres of which the youngest son, Edwin, and Art would each farm 800 acres. At the time, the Rudolph family farm was leased to Edwin who got married to Edna Wolf on June 2, 1948.

Our original plan was to live with them for the winter, but we changed our minds and decided to live in a vacant home on our own acreage. The Swartz home had not been occupied for many years. Matt Jr. and Ella lived there at one time, but left because there was not enough land for the family, the house roof leaked badly, there were lots of mice in it, and the foundation stood on rocks. The house was in such poor condition no one could live in it!

While Art and Edwin were preparing for the sale, Art's mother, Sophie, and I were cleaning, papering, painting, and patching two rooms at the house. We wanted them to be ready for winter living when we came back from our honeymoon trip out west.

Before the sale, Art had made arrangements with his father that he was going to bid and buy most of the machinery and some cattle. Art paid $5,600. at the sale and Matt carried him financially. Matt did not charge his children interest. This plan was very rewarding for us — we paid him back as we could afford it. Art bought twenty head of cattle at the sale. He had raised about fourteen head after he came back from the four years in the Army. I inherited six cows from my family, so we had a herd of approximately forty head.

The day of the sale, my parents, Helen and Julius Dockter, came to see where we were going to live. My mother said, "Any place to live is better than living with someone else. If hell breaks loose in the winter, where would they go then?"

The Honeymoon

After the sale, we left for our honeymoon which took us to Hardin, Montana, to visit the families of two of Art's sisters: Katie and Christ Kirschenman and Elvina and Emil Kirschenman. In Great Falls, Montana, we enjoyed a stay with my Aunt Lea and Uncle Ted Phiefle.

We made a stop at Pocatello, Idaho, to see Matt's younger brother, George Rudolph, and his family. Our trip went on to Yakima, Washington, where we stayed with my good friends, Milton and Katryn Schlepp. They were a delightful couple.

The next visit was with Art's sister, Emma, in Portland, Oregon. She had just gone through a major flood in Vancouver, Oregon (1948). She was living in a one-room suite with a half bath (shower and toilet stool). Emma lost everything she ever had. All she had left was the bathrobe she wore when they had to run for their lives. Some people ran bare naked because the authorities had unwisely lifted the flood threat two hours before the dam broke. She was overjoyed to see her brother and his bride! We stayed with her a week.

After we left Oregon, we went on to see beautiful, northern California.

Back to The Farm

The honeymoon was an exciting event for a seventeen-year-old. We came back home on Thanksgiving Day and stopped at my family farm. My father said to me, "How exciting that you have been in California! I'll bet you saw a lot."

We were still staying with our in-laws, Edwin and Edna. When we went to our new farm by Napoleon, we started moving in new furniture that my parents had given me: a green kitchen table and six chairs, a kitchen cabinet, a kitchen bottle gas stove, and a blond bedroom set.

There was no electricity, running water, bathroom, or telephone. My family home had electricity, a refrigerator, and a coal furnace. We had lived two miles from Venturia. Now I had to get used to shopping twenty miles away at Napoleon. I had a lot of experience housekeeping at age seventeen (I could run the household at age ten). Now, however, I had to learn to stock vital supplies. There was no way to preserve food — no refrigerator, basement or cellar, and not much time for cooking.

Our first winter after the honeymoon was a hard winter. We didn't need refrigeration then. I froze my feet and had to find a way to keep canned goods from freezing. The house we lived in was terrible. The area we lived in did not have graded roads. It was all section line road. We lived three miles from the State Highway 34 and did not get to town for six weeks at a time. After the snow was gone, "real life" began. We were farming 800 acres of land, milked ten cows by hand, and separated milk with hand-cranked separators. We also took care of forty head of range cattle. All these cattle were fed hay that was hand pitchforked – there was no other equipment available to us. Plus, we had a hog, chickens, geese, ducks, a cat, and a dog.

There were miles of barbed wire fence to repair. The farmland was run down because there had been no crop rotation. The fields were infested with wild oats, and quack grass had taken over. Most of the land was light soil and we farmed with used machinery.

The first spring we farmed, Art had constant breakdowns with his Oliver 99 Hart Par tractor because the governor was worn out. This had been a problem the year before we began farming. The governor was not repaired or replaced. In the meantime, I was taking care of all the chores. One morning at breakfast, Art said I was not feeding the cattle well. I started to cry and could not stop. I was at the breaking point and wished I could go home.

Our goal was not to get into debt. This motto was instilled in us by our parents. We were not going to pay any interest. There were many machine breakdowns and we did not have any hired help. The work always piled up and, as a result, I would milk ten cows in the morning and evening "by hand."

I had a garden which was located next to the windmill and well. The garden could be irrigated from the overflow of the stock tank. The garden was a paradise! There were so many vegetables; however, I did not have the time to preserve and can them. There was no electricity for freezing. I would put the vegetables in jars, but never had time to process them, so they usually spoiled.

In addition to all the farm work, there was our house which needed a new roof, plus a basement and foundation. The interior walls were lathe covered with a mixture of straw, clay, and cow manure. We lived in the house while all the inside walls were cleared of the covering. The wallpaper and clay were removed from the lathe. This was my first year of married life so...

Sophie and Matt Rudolph spent a lot of time on the farm the first year trying to get the house in a livable state. By fall, the roof had been repaired and the house was moved onto a half basement and foundation. Some of the windows were replaced and the walls were finished in wet plaster. This was all done while we lived in it!

All our woodwork was new. I did not get to finishing it until all the field work was done. My job was driving the tractor with the grain binder, doing summer fallow, cultivating corn, hauling grain, raking hay, etc.

By the time I got to finishing the new woodwork, the flies had plastered the wood with thousands of fly specks. In those days, new woodwork was a treasure — it was a crime to paint over it. Most of my time was spent digging fly specks out of the wood and finishing the woodwork.

The house was as cold as ever. There was no insulation to keep the wind out. After a lot of convincing, I got Art to buy a coal-fired heater that was placed in the basement. It had a register above the stove that brought the heat up to the kitchen. It was the first time that I had a place to stand on to warm my feet. We also had an oil heater.

In the winter months, we moved the bed into the living room, the warmest area of our house. This arrangement was okay until the fourth year we lived there. In 1952, our daughter, Jocelyn, joined the family. After that, we used the bedroom in the winter and repaired the two rooms upstairs for more bedrooms and storage.

We built our cattle herd to about sixty stock and ten milk cows. The spring of 1958, several cows aborted calves. The vet came and diagnosed the herd as infected with brucellosis ("Bang's disease") and reported it to the state Veterinary Department. We were subject to test the herd several times and had to sell our diseased cows and the suspects. After the disease had taken its toll, we had eighteen left out of a herd of seventy cows. We could not replace the cows because the farm was declared contaminated. At that time, it was hard to find Bangs vaccinated replacements. It took years to build a herd again!

In the tragedy of our herd depletion, there was a blessing: we lost the ten milk cows to Bangs and never replaced them. We missed the cream checks, but I did not miss the cows. I did not mind milking the cows, but getting the cows in the barn was another thing!

The cows were in a pasture that was a mile long. There was a slough lake that was half a mile long. Sometimes, they were in the other side of the slough. I thought they were on their way out, only to discover they changed their minds and went into the deep part of the slough. I was frustrated! I was not familiar with the lake and did not know the depth of the water. One time to get them out of the water, I got off the tractor and walked into the lake with my shoes on! As I found myself waist deep in the water, I discovered they had gotten out of the water and gone to the other side of the pasture!

The family farm where I grew up had a pasture beside the barn. By 6:00 p.m. the cows were waiting at the back of the barn. All we had to do was open the door and they walked into the barn.

My husband thought it was too early for me to quit in the field at 6:00 p.m. It was a drain on me to work in the field, go home at 7:00 p.m., round up the cows for one or two hours, and then milk ten cows. Most of the time, they did not milk well after chasing them for miles. I have often wondered how to get in touch with Spielberg and have him do a movie on "Ten Years of Hell Milking Ten Cows!"

After the Bang's disease had taken its toll on our herd of Herefords, we had to look at our situation and decide what direction our farming and our future would be. That same year (1958), Art's brother, Edwin, and his family of four boys decided to stop farming the other 800-acre farm. They moved to South Dakota and bought a farm there.

When I came into the community, we did not have any friends. This was hard for me to accept. The community I grew up in was a small-town community where everyone was either related or friends. We had lived in this farm community ten years and had a few friends in our church. Jocelyn was six now and had started public school. I started to teach Sunday School.

By this time, Grandfather Matt had experienced several strokes. His hopes were always high that Edwin would take over the farms. Now, Art was the only one left on the farms and he had only one girl. I had severe back problems by then.

The siblings in the Rudolph family felt that Grandfather Matt should sell the farms – that it was time to let go of the land. The first ten years we lived there, Grandfather was hard to get along with. Many times, when Grandfather and Art had differences, Grandfather would come to the farm and confront me with the problem. After several incidences, I became short with him because their disputes were not my concern. When it was obvious that we needed to buy the farm or move on, I did not want to buy the farm, and we started looking at other farms. However, we always came home, and I knew that Art did not want to leave the farm.

After Edwin went to South Dakota, we found out that Grandfather had leased Edwin's 800 acres to a Glatt family from Napoleon. Later that spring, the Glatt family decided they were not really interested in coming to that community. It was too far from town and their friends. They broke their lease which was for twelve months with no money down. Spring work was in progress by then. This was an opportunity for us. Art asked Grandfather Matt to crop share and rent the pasture, so we added 800 acres to the farm that we had leased for ten years.

We did not have good farm equipment. We were in the middle of sibling disputes about Grandfather Matt and our farming. The family bickering went on another two years. The family environment and my back problems became too much for me. My petition was either we buy, or we leave. One day, we were driving on Main Street at Napoleon and the banker, Mr. Heitman, waved for us to stop.

He said, "Why don't you kids buy your father's land? The finances are available, and you qualify."

We applied for an FHA loan. The loan was approved. There was one problem: FHA wanted our herd of Herefords and all the farm machinery for chattel mortgage. Art was not willing to do that because that was what happened to his father in the 30's and the results were not good. Grandfather Matt's land, livestock and machinery went into foreclosure. The farm sale bills were posted. One day before the sale, North Dakota Governor Langer called a moratorium on farm foreclosures. That saved the farm!

After Art would not allow a chattel mortgage, FHA said we would have to apply for a loan from three lending firms. If all three rejected our application, FHA would lend us the money for the land without a chattel mortgage.

The lending institutions they recommended were the Bank of North Dakota, Production Credit Association, and the Federal Land Bank. All three of them rejected our application for the purchase of the land without collateral, and FHA approved the loan. The loan covered the cost of 1,600 acres of land at $30. an acre and $10,000. for remodeling or building a new home.

2

DOCKTER FAMILY

Dockter Family, Ukraine To America

My grandfather, Gottlieb Dockter Jr., was born in Ukraine in 1866 and came to America when he was eighteen.

During the French Revolution, the German people living near the German French border were faced with starvation. They left and came to South Russia, Ukraine.

Eventually, times became difficult in Neudorf, Ukraine (an area near the Black Sea). After Katherine the Great was no longer in power, the Germans that came from Germany lost all the freedom and privileges that were granted to them. They were no longer exempt from the military horrors of fighting against the Turks that were a constant threat to the Ukraine. Some families were so desperate to keep their boys out of the military service that they dressed them in girls' clothes to disguise them. Sometimes they could keep their gender a secret until the boys were almost fully mature.

The Russians made farming hard for them, always demanding more production, imposing fines and taxes that were impossible to pay, and confiscating more and more from them. Eventually, they were no better off than when they had to leave their homes and farms in Strasburg, Germany.

After going through these hard times, several purges, drought and no crops, Russian governmental control, and constant threat of war, they looked for a way to escape to America.

The Gottlieb Dockter Sr. family chose to take the train somewhere in Ukraine and traveled to the Hamburg seaport in northern Germany. They boarded the steamship, "EMS" and sailed to America arriving on May 16, 1885.

After port clearance at Ellis Island, they took the train across the United States to Yankton, South Dakota. From there they went north to Tripp, South Dakota, and later to Eureka, South Dakota, in search of land to claim a homestead. Their search ended two miles north of the state line at Venturia, North Dakota. Gottlieb Dockter Sr. filed a homestead claim one and a half miles north of Venturia.

By then, Gottlieb Dockter Jr. was married to Eva Lehr (born in 1866). Gottlieb Dockter Sr. and his son, Gottlieb Jr., had homesteaded and built sod houses about one quarter of a mile apart. Gottlieb Jr.'s oldest son was also named Gottlieb G. Eva gave birth to three more children who died in infancy. She died of childbirth when her last child was born in 1894. Gottlieb G. was their surviving child. Eva and the three babies were buried on the farmstead near the sod house and other farm buildings.

On February 5, 1895, Gottlieb Dockter Jr. married Christina Villhauer (born in 1878). It must have been a difficult life for a young bride of seventeen to begin married life with a young son, plus all the hardships of a pioneer woman. Christina and Gottlieb Jr. had five boys: Albert, Emil, Julius, Leopold and Edwin. They had five girls: Eva, Magdalena, Christina, Lea and Ella. One girl was diagnosed as a spina bifida baby and died at birth.

Records of Childhood Family

My father, Julius Dockter, was born in 1906. My mother, Helen Esch, was born in 1909. I was born in 1931 in two-room farmhouse two miles north of Venturia, North Dakota. This was one mile north of the homestead claim of my grandfather, Gottlieb Dockter Jr., where my father, Julius, was born in a sod house. My parents married in 1926.

My mother, Helena Esch Dockter and father Julius Dockter had seven children:
Florence Pearl, born in 1927 (deceased),
LeRoy, born in 1929, (deceased)
Florence Helen, born in 1931,
Inez Eunice, born in 1936,
Stanley Julius, born in 1938 (deceased),
Gladys Grace, born in 1941,
Stanley Roger, born in 1945.

Grandfather Gottlieb Dockter Jr. Man Of Wisdom (Part 1)

Grandfather Gottlieb Dockter Jr. was a man of wisdom. He was a studious, knowledgeable, and religious person. He was eighteen years old when he came to America. He filed a homestead patent claim at Bismarck, North Dakota, on July 8, 1903. The homestead certificate number was 4752 and was signed by President Theodore Roosevelt.

Great-grandfather Gottlieb Dockter Sr. came to America in 1885 and filed a preemption patent at Aberdeen, South Dakota, on October 14, 1891. The certificate number was 9873 and was signed in testimony by President Benjamin Harrison. These two claims were in the section of land located one and half miles north of Venturia, North Dakota. This was a great advantage for our grandfather, Gottlieb Jr., to live next door to his father, Gottlieb Sr. It is at this location that they each built a sod house. They were the first settlers to break the sod. There were no fences or trees. All they had were rocks and sod.

Since Venturia had not been founded in 1889, they had to travel for supplies by oxen or horse to either Ashley, North Dakota (founded in 1888), or Eureka, South Dakota (founded in 1884). The first thing they did was to erect a house and a barn. The walls were made of sod. The roofs, windows, and doors were made of lumber which was hauled from the Missouri River by oxen with the old-fashioned yoke across their necks. Oxen were used for difficult tasks like pulling the wagons and plows. Digging a well for water was also a big task.

Sod houses were warm in the winter and cool in the summer. Sometimes, settlers built large sod houses and used half for family housing and the other half for cows, horses, and other animals. The animals gave out body heat which helped them when they had a blizzard storm with forty degrees below with the windchill factor.

We have a lot of information about Grandfather Gottlieb Jr. and his ownership of Belgian draft horses. He had so much pride in them. We know that in the first years, he worked with oxen to farm the land. Logic tells us that oxen were much stronger for plowing and turning sod. Turning sod was the first step to seeding wheat. The Dakota area was the greatest producer of spring wheat. Eureka, South Dakota, was the shipping point after the railroad was laid.

Grandfather Gottlieb Jr. could see into the future and had already provided for his children. He helped them through the economic crash of 1929 (a time when no one had any money), the drought of the 1930s, and the locusts of 1938.

The severe drought caused a shortage of hay and feed. It was hard to put up enough hay to feed the horses and cattle. Many farmers were put out of business after they had to sell or give away their livestock.

I remember my parents mentioning a debt of $3000. I was about eight years old when I said, "What was that money for?"

Mother said it was money to buy hay and to buy seed for spring seeding. They did not have to sell more cattle.

Dear Grandma, Gottlieb Dockter Jr., Farmer, Generous

Dear Grandma Katie,

Grandfather Gottlieb Jr. was a bonanza farmer. World War I took place before 1918. At that time, most of his sons were not military draft age. Therefore, they did not serve in the military service.

There was some money to be made farming in the 1920's. Grandfather built an eighty-foot cattle and horse barn. He owned forty draft horses.

He, with his six sons, farmed a sizeable number of acres of crop land. The result was acreage of approximately fifteen quarter sections of land.

After his sons were twenty-one years of age, he gave them each 160 acres of land with the farm buildings, and another 160 acres of land which he expected them to pay him back for his retirement. In addition, he gave them a complete set of farm machinery, four work horses (complete with new harnesses), a cream separator, 100 pounds of flour, some sugar, plus many other items to set up farming and a household.

He gave each of his three oldest daughters 160 acres of land, six milk cows, and a complete line of household furniture. He compensated his two youngest daughters with homes and money.

At the end of the twenties, he was considered a wealthy man. However, after the crash of 1929, with several years of drought, he bankrupted and applied for welfare. He had given all his land away. Because of the economy, he was never paid back. The end result was he died a poor man. Grandfather gave my parents a farmhouse, a place to put a pillow under our heads, and we never had to move.

During my childhood, we visited him often. His house was a one and a half story house. We were never allowed to go up the stairs. It was later in life that I found out that he had stored his coffin in a room upstairs. He had arranged his funeral complete with the purchase of a coffin.

He was a man who believed in God and had a strong faith in the resurrection. He leaned on the arms of his Savior, Jesus Christ.

Note: Grandfather was a kind and generous father. He also demanded a lot of work from his children and taught them a great deal about life. He was respected by his family and community.

Dear Grandma, Mother Helen, Youth

Dear Grandma Katie,

Times must have been very hard for you sometimes. Your oldest daughter, Helen (my mother) was taken out of your home when she was thirteen because of her stepfather's behavior. She went to Ashley to live with her grandfather, Johann Helfenstein Sr., and her grandmother. Grandfather Johann Sr. hired her to farmers in the surrounding

15

community. She was assigned to chores on the farm, yard work, housekeeping, and caring for children. She also did field work. She learned how to harrow, seed drill, and disc with a team of four horses.

My mother did housework and babysitting in the homes of Albert and Lydia Dockter, and Emil and Albina Dockter. In 1926, she was hired to the Gottlieb Jr. and Christina (Villhauer) Dockter home to help care for Christina who was terminally ill at the time.

A few years earlier, Christina had a hysterectomy which was done by two doctors, the Merckline twins. One of the Dr. Merckline twins had an office in Ashley, North Dakota, and his twin brother was a doctor in Oaks, North Dakota. Both doctors assisted in the surgery at the office in Oaks, North Dakota. Gottlieb Jr., her husband, was present. My mother told me the surgery was performed on an examination table. One of the doctors was monitoring her pulse by holding her wrist. The operation was successful, but her diagnosis and prognosis were not discussed. The exact year is not known.

In early summer of 1926, she had surgery for gall bladder at Bismarck, North Dakota, and was diagnosed with terminal cancer. It was in this situation that my mother was hired into the Dockter home which was her future in-law family. Helen was seventeen years old and took care of Christina. She also cooked and did all the household duties for a family of five siblings and Gottlieb Jr. My grandfather knew that Helen was a good cook.

Grandmother knew that her son, Julius, and Helen were planning to get married and asked for their marriage take place at the foot of her deathbed. It was a fulfilling wish for Grandmother Christina, but it was not a blessing to the beginning of their marriage.

The story about the surgery the twin doctors Merckline performed on Christina Dockter is as it was told to my mother, Helen, and Aunt Christina Bauman by my grandfather, Gottlieb Dockter Jr. Her diagnosis was cancer. In those days, little was spoken about cancer. It was considered an evil curse.

Grandfather Gottlieb Dockter Jr. Man Of Wisdom (Part 2)

I had to be in my mother's presence to do whatever needed to be done. I asked a lot of questions, and one day she explained about debt. During the depression and drought, farmers could borrow money from the government. This "Feed and Seed" loan saved a lot of farmers!

It needed to be paid back. However, the payback never happened. The only clue I ever had about that loan was when my father sold his farm in 1964. My brother, LeRoy, was a Certified Public Accountant. He stated that there was a $500 tax due for the "Feed and Seed" loan made by the United States government in the 1930s. My brother is not here to answer questions now, so we don't have any more information.

Gottlieb Jr. made another land purchase after he had given his farmland to the family. The location was on the south side of Venturia. It was swampland – – low land that flooded after the heavy snow thawed. After the water evaporated and the soil dried out, tall lake hay grew. The land was dry enough in the late summer to bale hay. Grandfather had an agreement that all his sons could make and share the hay which was suitable for horses. There were about 320 acres in that slough. I remember our father got a good-sized stack each year. In 1937, he received a smaller hayrack full of hay. Grandfather bought the land from the Weidman brothers who owned the hardware store that had the post office in it in Venturia, North Dakota.

I vaguely remember going to the slough when my parents were making hay. The reason I remember is because my mother packed the lunch. I must have been about three or four years old.

I see Grandfather's plan when he bought the land that was considered swamp. The hay that came from that lake helped his sons provide feed for their horses during the drought! That swamp area is completely flooded at the present time and may never become productive again.

Grandfather Dockter had quality draft horses. My father, Julius, received four of these horses in his dowry. Two were matched black mares, Queen and Beauty. Dolly was chestnut brown with a black mane and tail. Her pair was a white mare whose name was Fly.

From Sod House To Wood House

Grandfather Dockter made plans to build a new house and a new barn. He wanted to move out of his sod house and construct a new, wooden home for his large family of eleven children. We don't know if his new house was a Sears' prefabricated house that was shipped in by rail or if it was built by a carpenter. Settlers usually had a surprise when they moved out of their thick-walled sod house into a thin-walled wooden house. Fortunately, Grandfather had some knowledge about insulation.

His son, Edwin, eventually inherited the homestead and farmed there with his family. After many years, he retired, and the house was sold and moved. When they raised the house to put it on timbers, the movers discovered that it was insulated from the floor sill up to the windows with ashes! That was good insulation — there was nothing that could destroy ashes. This solid home stood in that location for over fifty years. When the house was moved, it was restored to good condition and still stands in Wishek, North Dakota.

The barn he built was about eighty feet long. It was large enough to house forty draft horses and the milk cows. The side lean may have housed the sheep and hogs.

Grandfather Gottlieb Dockter Jr., Venturia Home

I have always been fascinated with Grandfather Gottlieb Jr. and his home in Venturia. The home was built by one of the Kretchmar families. According to my mother, they had an interior designer come from Bismarck, North Dakota. It was quite new when Grandfather purchased it.

The décor was unique in its time. The walls throughout were a gold color textured, design with a deep blue ½" border around all the doors and windows. 9 x 12 Persian wool area rugs covered the hardwood floors in the dining and living rooms. This luxury was uncommon in most homes at that time.

When my parents went to Venturia to do their business, we would stop in to drop off some cream, milk and eggs. Grandfather was a diabetic. His diet was soft boiled eggs and rye bread. I do not know if he baked his own bread. Perhaps one of his daughters baked his bread.

Sometimes, we stayed with Grandfather while our parents did business uptown. Every time we came to visit him, he took us into the living room by his easy chair and leather sofa. He sat in his chair, took his Bible, and told us if we would sit and listen to him read the Bible a few minutes, he would look around and see if we could find some candy. He shared the candy with us and gave each one of us either a penny or a nickel. We could buy an all-day candy sucker for one penny. For a nickel, we could buy either a cone of ice cream, bottle of pop, or a candy bar.

His yard was always neat and clean. His yard was fenced with a welded wire and wooden posts. The top of the wire was topped with a 2 x 4 laid on top of the posts. It was quite sturdy because we tried to walk on it.

Dear Grandma, Grandfather Dockter Driving Car, 1929 Financial Crash

Dear Grandma Katie,

Grandfather Dockter lived independently in his home until he was eighty-three. He had a large yard to care for and used a hand-pushed lawn mower (no motor). He owned a 1938 Ford which was a burgundy color with a white convertible top. It was a fashionable car in its day. At that time, most state roads were gravel topped. It was fun to see our grandfather drive at high speed down the road past our farmyard in a cloud of dust. He always seemed to be in a hurry.

Grandfather taught his daughter, Christine, to drive the car when she was a teenager. He saw the value and need for transportation. In those days, most women never learned how to drive. Our family was fortunate because our mother could drive the car. She also knew how to maintain it by having the oil changed and a grease job done.

Grandfather Dockter had given all his land and property to his children, but there were no crops because dust storms and droughts had taken their toll on farmers. There was, however, one more threat coming up on the horizon of which no one had ever heard or understood. It was

19

the financial crash of 1929. The dollar lost its value. Banks closed. The government could not function without money. Grain lost its value — a bushel of grain did not have enough value to cover shipping costs. Eventually, land lost its value. The banks did not want the land either. The North Dakota governor, Langer, called a moratorium on farm foreclosures. Everything lost its value.

Grandfather Dockter had become a poor man and had to apply for welfare assistance. He warned his sons never to mortgage their land and to always pay the taxes.

We always stopped to visit Grandfather Dockter. He did not allow us to go upstairs in his house. We found out about his secret after he died. He had stored his coffin upstairs.

Ukranish Baptismal Cap

There were eleven children in my father's family of Gottlieb Dockter Jr. They were Gottlieb Dockter (son of Grandfather's first wife, Eva Lehr), Eva, Magdalena, Christine, Albert, Emil, Julius, Leopold, Edwin, Lea, and Ella (ten children of Grandfather Dockter Jr.'s second wife, Christina Villhauer).

Some of the older children in the family received a baptismal cap for their firstborn from Magdalena Villhauer. The one my father and mother received was handknit of silk yarn and is a colorful, unique piece of art. There are rows of flowers. Glass beads were used to form flower designs and each bead had to be strung in the correct order before knitting began. It took hundreds, perhaps thousands, of beads to make this amazing cap. When finished, close examination showed there was not one place where the thread was broken in the design.

My father was the last member of the Dockter family to receive a baptismal cap, and I was baptized in it. It was on exhibit at the first family reunion in Bismarck, North Dakota. After much discussion, there was not another family relative who could remember such a cap in their family.

I received this baptismal cap from my parents, Helen and Julius Dockter. It may have been made in Ukraine and is over 100 years old.

I framed it in a 12 x 12-inch box frame, and later consigned it to the North Dakota State Historical Museum.

The Historic Book

The Dockter Family Of German From Russia Heritage

This is a historic book compiled by LeRoy Dockter. Hundreds of Dockter descendants cooperated with information needed to record the 2,400 descendants who lived lives of hard work.

We were fortunate that our ancestors located in America! We could enjoy the freedom that no other country could offer: freedom to choose, freedom to worship, to work, to rest, to find a job, to build a house (a small house or large house), to buy a new car or an old car, to save money or spend money, to choose a profession: to be a teacher, a preacher, a farmer, to work for a company, or to be a garbage hauler, to buy property, to lease property.

There is no other country that offers the freedom that we have! Our ancestors laid the groundwork for us.

Dear Grandma, Christian Dockter, Bone Setter, Chiropractor

Dear Grandma Katie,

Do you remember Christian, our great uncle? He was a younger brother of my grandfather, Gottlieb Dockter Jr. He was a self-trained, bone setter and chiropractor. He could put dislocated joints in place, set compound fractures, and do spinal adjustments.

He began in the early 1900's. His practice and treatments were in Wishek, North Dakota, but people came to him from long distances. In the early years of his practice, he did not have modern appliances to set compound fractures. He used wooden shingles, and his procedures were accurate and usually successful. Occasionally, there was a problem with infection.

Since Christian did not have a license for his practice, the local medical doctor and a licensed chiropractor took him to court to try to put him out of business.

People kept coming to him and pleading with him to set their injured bones and ease their pain. Christian treated them; however, he could not take any money for his service. They bartered and gave him beef, chickens, farm products, and many other material things that he needed.

The medical doctor and chiropractor could see that it was not possible to put Christian out of business. Since they could not lick him, they joined him. The medical doctor administered anesthesia and penicillin for setting compound fractures, and the chiropractor did x-rays when necessary. This made Christian's practice more effective than ever. The trio organized a team, and everyone was happy. Christian practiced until he was about seventy years old, and was known as the bone setter.

Dear Grandma, Phillip Dockter, California

Dear Grandma Katie,

Phillip Dockter was a younger brother in the Gottlieb Dockter Sr. family, and was the most adventurous one. During the Depression in 1929, he traveled to the Lodi, California, area to invest in a winery. He lived there the remainder of his life, and his family grew up in that community.

Phillip was always in touch with my grandfather, Gottlieb Jr. He shipped several boxes of apples to him every fall (usually the Winesap variety), and would also ship a box of Red Delicious apples for Christmas.

During the year, Grandfather would order a wooden barrel of grape juice which was shipped by rail. He followed instructions on how to tap it, added the correct amount of sugar and yeast for fermentation, and sealed the barrel until the process was complete. Everyone was served a small glass of wine for breakfast as an appetizer.

Dear Grandma, Admiration and Courage

Dear Grandma Katie,

My aunt, Leah Dockter Pheifle, was born on December 25, 1913. She was taken out of school at ten years of age when her mother, Christina Villhauer Dockter, became ill. She later married Theodore Pheifle. When he passed away in 1960, she found herself as a widow with seven children. She was forty-seven years old when she had to support a family and go back to school. With little formal education, she put herself through school in the field of nursing.

She moved to Great Falls, Montana, and worked for twenty-five years as a licensed practical nurse. She was a courageous, hard-working person. She worked in a hospital delivery room as an assistant until her retirement. I admired her and remember her as a jolly, fun loving aunt.

Dear Grandma, Christine Gifted A Washing Machine

Dear Grandma Katie,

Some things that went unnoticed were really significant in their time. Christine Bauman, my father's older sister, married into a wealthy family and received a new washing machine from her husband's relatives.

She gave my parents her used washing machine as a wedding gift. At that time, they could not afford a new one. It was a godsend for my mother!

3

Helfenstein Family

Ancestry, Maternal

<u>Maternal Great Grandparents</u>
Johann (John) Helfenstein
Karolina Wenz

<u>Maternal Grandparents</u>
Heinrich (Henry) Esch
Katharina (Katie) Helfenstein

<u>Parents</u>
Julius Dockter
Helena (Helen) Esch

<u>Maternal Great Grandparents</u>
Johann (John) Helfenstein
Born September 9, 1851, Groszliebental, Russia
Died March 10, 1936, Ashley, North Dakota

Karolina Wenz
Born April 26, 1857, Gildendorf, Russia
Died December 6, 1937, Ashley, North Dakota

Maternal Grandparents
Heinrich (Henry) Esch
Born November 26, 1884, Romania
Died November 10, 1918, Emmons County, North Dakota (Gimbel
Gayton Cemetery)
Married July 11, 1908, Hazelton, North Dakota

Katharina (Katie) Helfenstein
Born February 18, 1889, Luinka (Odessa) Bessarabia, Russia
Died May 29, 1970, Minneapolis, Minnesota

Parents
Julius Dockter
Born May 3, 1906, Venturia, North Dakota (rural)
Died September 11, 1976

Helena (Helen) Esch
Born March 25, 1909, Hazelton, North Dakota
Died March 26, 1994, Minneapolis, Minnesota

Dear Grandma, Helfenstein Family, Ship To America, Settled In North Dakota

Dear Grandma Katie,
   The name of the ship that brought you to America was the Kaiser
Frederich. It sailed from Bremen, Germany, on November 18, 1897.
According to the list or manifest, the following family members were
on the ship:

Name	Age	
Johann (John) Helfenstein	47	
Karolina Helfenstein	41	
Margarita Helfenstein	21	(wife of Johann Jr.)
Karolina (Carrie) Helfenstein	20	(Little Maggie's mother)
Johann (John) Helfenstein	19	
Jacob Helfenstein	15	(died in Flu of 1918)
Juliania Helfenstein	10	
Katharina (Katie) Helfenstein	8	

Their destination was Eureka, South Dakota, and the total fare was $267. Later, they went north in search of land to the Dawson area of North Dakota and settled there. I do not know if they claimed a homestead.

Dear Grandma, Ages Of Your Children When Your First Husband Died

Dear Grandma Katie,

Your first husband, Heinrich (Henry) Esch, died in an influenza epidemic on November 10, 1918. He was my grandfather whom I never met.

When he died, these were the ages of your children:

Name	Birthdate	Age	
Helena (Helen) Esch	1909	10	(my mother)
Carrie Esch	1911	9	
Edyth Esch			
Andrew Esch	1914	3	
Edna Esch	1918		

Dear Grandma, From Germany To Ukraine, Then To America

Dear Grandma Katie,

It must have been hard for your parents to leave Germany and go to a strange, unsettled land like Ukraine. Your mother was a midwife in Ukraine, and later in the United States. She said she was glad to see a baby boy being born, but sad to see a baby girl being born. Because childbirth was so difficult, many first-time mothers died in childbirth. Or, soon they had many babies, and it was difficult to support and care for them. My mother told me her grandmother delivered over 1000 babies in her lifetime.

You told me you were only eight years old when you came to America. It must have been very different when you lived in Ukraine, or as you called it, "South Russia". Your mother said people lived in small villages or dorfs together and had their gardens and animals near them. The women and children were in the villages while the fathers went into the surrounding fields, and then came back to the dorf at night.

Great Grandparents' Home, Yard, City Cow

As a six year old, I vaguely remember the little house in Ashley, North Dakota, where my great grandfather and great grandmother Helfenstein lived. It was a small house with a lean-to on one side and a little porch on the other. The lean-to had a long kitchen with a cupboard and cookstove. There was a lid in the floor which could be lifted. It opened to the steps that went down into the cellar. There were no windows in the cellar, so Great Grandmother would light a lantern to go down and find what she needed. There was a potato bin, a barrel of sauerkraut, a barrel or can of flour, a barrel of salt pork, a barrel of pickles and pickled watermelon, and some canned goods.

The main part of the home was a living room and bedroom combined. There was a bed, rocking chair, some small tables for plants, a large parlor heater, and a table where they put the kerosene light.

The backyard was so fascinating. The entire yard was planted as a vegetable garden with potatoes, carrots, beets, cabbage, and about

everything that grew in North Dakota. There were also a few flowers that Grandfather thought were unnecessary. The well had a hand pump on it and was used for water in the house and for watering the garden.

There was a small shed with a little fence around it where the cow stayed. Their cow produced milk and cream for butter and cheese. Grandfather's son, Johann, always supplied a cow for his parents' needs. Grandfather's city cow ate hay and anything else they gave her. She fed on the garbage such as vegetable and potato peels, dry bread, and left-over scraps from the table. She even drank the milk that was not needed for household use. We were so fascinated by what she ate. It was fun to watch her feed.

Dear Grandma, Uncle Johann Jr. Farm

Dear Grandma Katie,

Visiting the farm of Uncle Johann Helfenstein Jr. was always an adventure. His farm was located fifteen miles east of Ashley, North Dakota. Our farm was nine miles west of Ashley. That was approximately twenty-five miles. Highway 11 was a gravel road at that time, and it was a long way to drive in a 1933 Whippit car. I do not know how fast a car like that moved, but it seemed a long time of motoring to the Coldwater store. Then we turned North and went about three miles to get to the farm.

The house was fairly roomy and not very old. There was a main floor and some bedrooms upstairs. The floors were hardwood with no finish on them and looked as though they were impossible to keep clean. The time period was in the late thirties when no one had money to do anything – not even to buy floor varnish.

Everything about those visits is vague to me. What I enjoyed most was visiting the two youngest girls, Hilda and Edna. They had a room upstairs and would ask me to their room and doll me up. They polished my fingernails, applied lipstick, showed me how to walk in their high heels, and curled my hair. Edna lit a kerosene lamp and held a metal curling iron into the lamp chimney until it was hot. Then they removed it and curled my hair. It felt good to be treated so kindly. No one had ever been so kind to me.

Not long ago, Hilda told me about her parents, Johann and Margaret. The first house they owned had a chimney fire and burned to the ground. Eleven young children lived in that small house — two boys and nine girls. None of the household could be salvaged. Most of the neighbors had large families, but they took the children into their homes. They also hosted the parents until they had a home. Johann then purchased a house and moved it to the farm.

Life for Johann's daughters was very hard. He used them on the farm like hired men. They had to hoe and weed the field corn. The land he farmed was rough – a lot of hills loaded with rocks of all sizes. The rocks had to be dug and picked by hand. After the girls had picked the larger rocks, they had to pick the small ones with a pail or even in their aprons. There was a large lake in one of the fields. Johann's plan was to dig a canal and drain the lake into another field. The girls had to dig the trench using picks and spades. Sometimes there was a question: was it the benefit of the work or was it a form of control and punishment that he forced upon his daughters?

His wife, Margaret, had a hard life. Despite her bearing ten children for him, he made it clear that she had to be out there in the fields and do the same work as the others did. He did not want her to wear a white scarf so the neighbors would see her working. She was a petite, mild-mannered lady. At that time, she was about forty-five years old. Her hair was thin, always neatly pulled back in a bun. Her hands showed hard work. She did not have any teeth.

Johann also did some ranching with cattle and sheep. One morning, he loaded some sheep to take to the sale in Fargo, North Dakota. While they were loading, things did not work as he had planned. The girls were helping him, but Hilda had a sore, bandaged arm. Because of her injury, she could not help with the work. He beat her severely with a chain. After he was gone, Hilda was so hurt and angry, she said, "I hope he never comes back."

On the way to Fargo with the truckload of sheep, he was in an accident and got killed. After his death, life was not any better on the farm for the girls. In fact, it was even harder. After a few years, Aunt Margaret had an auction sale where she sold all her property and farmland.

Dear Grandma, Death of Johann Helfenstein Jr.

Johann Helfenstein Jr.
Born October 4, 1878, Elsas (Odessa) Bessarabia, Russia
Died December 24, 1937

Dear Grandma Katie,

Johann was your brother.

I remember that evening when our family was in the kitchen. As usual, we were sitting around the table with the kerosene lamp the only light in the room. Our dog started to bark, and we saw a car in the yard. It was our mother's cousin, Albertina Helfenstein. She was married to Mr. Shock, and they lived in the western part of North Dakota. They were on their way to the Helfenstein family farm east of Ashley.

They had some bad news. Her father, Johann Helfenstein Jr., was killed in a truck accident the day before Christmas, December 24. The funeral was to be the next day. They said the plan was to have all the granddaughters and daughters of cousins at any age carry flowers. When they left, they said, "The funeral will be tomorrow. Please bring Florence."

My mother said, "Yes."

The funeral was December 27, 1937. I was six years old on October 17, 1937. The next morning when we got up, I asked my mother, "Which dress well I wear for the funeral?"

She said, "You won't go along. You are staying at home with the baby."

I cried. Inez was eighteen months old. I was so upset. I don't remember anything about that day other than being alone. I was six years old. I didn't know where my brother, LeRoy, was. I didn't know when my parents were coming home that night.

The funeral was at Coldwater which was seventeen miles east of Ashley. Our farm was nine miles west of Ashley. That was a total of twenty-six miles from our home. This was in December. We only had coal stoves. I don't remember if we were cold, if LeRoy went to school, or if we had something to eat. There were no telephones, no TV, no toys. I never had a doll. I don't think I knew anything about a radio. All I knew was that when my mother came home, she said to me, "They waited for you at the funeral." I cried some more.

Dear Grandma, Lost On A Foggy Day

Dear Grandma Katie,

I am sure life was very hard in Ukraine, but it must have been difficult to leave everything behind and go to a strange, new country. I am sure you had many friends who were dear to you. Your trip on the ship to America must have been adventurous, but frightening.

I do not know where you lived when you came to North Dakota. One place was on a farm south of Dawson, North Dakota. It was there when your father, John Helfenstein Sr., told you to walk to Dawson and buy some smoking tobacco for him.

It was a very foggy day. There were no roads, and you got lost. Your mother said to your father, "If that child does not survive, I will never forgive you for sending her to town because of your smoking tobacco." A search party found you.

Times must have been very lonely living on a homestead claim with no neighbors within miles. Life in Ukraine was very controlled, however, living in a Dorf offered a lot of companionship for the women and children.

Dear Grandma, Grandpa Esch —1918 Influenza

Dear Grandma Katie,

You told me about the time in 1918 when you lived on a farm near Hazleton, North Dakota. You and Grandpa Henry Esch had five children: my mother, Helen (age ten), Carrie, Ida, Andrew, and baby Edna. Edna was ten months old when Grandpa Henry died of the 1918 Influenza.

It was November when he died. You were left on the farm with five little children and winter was coming. How could you manage the farm during those winter months?

The influenza had taken its toll with many people dying. There was no one who had the health or energy to take care of the sick, no one to bury the dead, no one well enough to dig the graves, and no clergy available for funerals.

The body of Grandpa Henry was lying in state in an unheated bedroom in your home. You lived in that same house with your five children until spring when a funeral was possible. During those winter months, Ida, who was about seven or eight years old, would sneak into the bedroom to lie beside her father. He had been dead for some time. It must have been a comfort to her to know he was still there. It became a frequent event, and you decided to put a lock on the door so she could not go into the room anymore. The pain and hardships must have been unending for you!

My Great Grandparents Helfenstein

Karolina Helfenstein was a tall, strong woman. Her face had deep lines and her hands were gnarled from her hard life and the demanding work she did. Grandfather seemed to be a stern man. I don't remember Grandmother being dressed in her Sunday best. Most of the time, she was wearing a casual, calico dress with an apron to keep her dress clean. She was a very kind, mild-mannered person, and was always ready to share what she had.

Grandmother and Grandfather did not have a car. Whenever someone asked them to go along for a visit somewhere, Grandmother always took along a loaf of bread just in case there was a need for it. In those days, there was no bread to be bought.

Grandfather was so independent. For example, when there was a large group eating at the table, he would not ask someone to pass the food. He would stand up and reach for whatever he wanted. One time, he stood up to get what he wanted to eat. As he stood up, his granddaughter, Carrie, pulled his chair up to the cupboard to reach for something. When Grandfather sat down, he missed the chair and went crashing down to the floor. There were some mixed emotions when he was getting up from the floor. There were some real concerns about his being hurt, but there was also the humorous side for those that could not keep a straight face. Fortunately, he was not hurt. I don't know if this broke him of his habit. (I'm the only one of my siblings that remember Karolina and John Helfenstein Sr. and where they lived.)

Carrie lived with her grandparents in Ashley after she had to leave her uncle's home. She was a small person, not quite five feet tall. A sweet, little lady and one of the favorite aunts. She had small hands and small feet, a size 3½ shoe that was very hard to find. Her feet always hurt because her shoes were not wide enough. When I was about eight years old, she would give me her new shoes to break them in for her. Sometimes, they were almost worn out by the time she got them back because she lived approximately seventy miles from where we lived. Aunt Carrie and my mother, Helen, had such a good time reminiscing about the time when they were growing up and when Carrie came to visit my parents before she got married to Uncle Ben.

My father, Julius, was an innovative person. He was always planning some handy gadgets to make life better. One year, he harvested the pumpkins and stored them in our tiny cellar. He did not want them on the cement floor, so he tied strings around the stems and suspended them from the floor beams in the cellar. It was about that time, when Mother and her sister, Carrie, were listening to the phonograph playing polka music. They polkaed so hard, the kitchen floor shook and the stems on the pumpkins let loose! The pumpkins dropped and smashed on the concrete floor in the cellar. That was one of father's favorite stories and he told it many times. There was not much pumpkin to eat that year.

Dear Grandma, The Truth…You Are Loved

Dear Grandma Katie,

When you lived in the Dawson area, your older sister, Karolina (Great Aunt Carrie) worked at the hotel in Dawson. She met an Englishman,

Elmer Hopkins, and later married him. Elmer was teaching school at the time. After they started a family, the Hopkins family moved to a farm near Pettibone.

Great Aunt Carrie was an expressive person. Some of the relatives made fun of her heavy accent when she spoke. I feel she did well because she spoke both German and Russian when she came to America. She soon mastered the English language as well. During the time she and her large family lived in the Pettibone area, she would take the train and go to Ashley to visit her parents, Johann and Karolina Helfenstein.

Shortly after the Helfenstein family came to America, Carrie, the oldest child of the Helfenstein family (age twenty), gave birth to a little girl named Maggie. Carrie was not married. At the time, it was convenient for her mother, Karolina Helfenstein, to claim little Maggie as her own child. No one in the family knew that Carrie was little Maggie's mother.

Little Maggie was a very pretty girl and became engaged to John Gimbel. A few days before the wedding, Grandmother Karolina met with Maggie and John to tell her that Carrie Hopkins was her mother. Maggie did not show any emotion.

John said, "I will always love Maggie no matter what. I always thought Karolina Helfenstein was too old to have a girl Maggie's age."

At Carrie and Elmer Hopkins' 50th wedding anniversary, the photographer arranged their family of a dozen children to take pictures. Elmer insisted that Maggie Gimbel be in the family picture. Carrie looked shocked and another member removed Maggie. However, Elmer said, "Maggie belongs on the picture." Elmer knew the truth and little Maggie was on the picture.

Dear Grandma, Widow, Moved To Be Near Parents

Dear Grandma Katie,

I do not know much about your life between the time you were eight years old and when you married Henry Esch. After you were married, you lived close to Hazleton, North Dakota, and had five children.

My mother was your oldest child. When your husband died in the 1918 Flu, she was ten years old.

Times were very hard for you with five young children. You tell us of the way you took in laundry and ironing and did some housecleaning for other people. Sometimes, your children did not have overshoes to wear when they walked to country school, and many times your children went to bed hungry.

After the loss of your husband, you tried to farm for a year. But you sold your farm the next year. After that, you moved to be closer to your parents who lived in Ashley, North Dakota.

My Grandma Katie

My Grandma Katie was an attractive lady. She was tall, slender hipped, had long slender hands and beautiful hair. She showed a lot of pride in how she dressed. She loved cleanliness and her home was neat and orderly. Though she appreciated fine things like China and glassware, she could not afford these luxuries.

She did general housecleaning. As she cleaned, she was constantly admiring the nice things people had in their China closets. Many of these clients respected her for the good work she did. Sometimes, they would say they wanted to give away or clean some of these little treasures and offered them to her. She eventually had a collection of many beautiful and precious items.

I remember her beautiful China dishes, copper pitchers and glasses, carnival glass, and depression glass. I feel that is why I appreciate some of the China and treasures I have.

Dear Grandma, Rain Would Have Saved Everything

Dear Grandma Katie,

The first memories I have are, "If only it would rain." My mother described the pasture as "bare as the kitchen table." I was four years old.

This was 1935. It was the middle of the Dust Bowl years. It was about the time the government came up with "Feed and Seed Loans." (I

35

explained that procedure in another article.) That loan saved the horses from being sold. Horses were the main source of power for farming. All the equipment was built for horsepower. Tractors were not available, affordable, or suitable for farm equipment. Many farmers were short of grain and hay and had to sell their milk cows for a "giveaway price." The sale of milk and cream was the only salable product they had.

The Orphan Train

In America between 1854 and 1943, trains transported over 200,000 orphans from the east to the west where they became residents. Many train riders did not know about the orphan train. Some who did understand thought there was only one orphan train.

Who were these orphans? During the period of 1929 to 1943, they were children roaming the streets of eastern cities. It was common that orphans had a father who had died and mother who was institutionalized. Some parents had abandoned them during the drought and financial crash in the economy of 1929. Thousands of people stood in soup lines and were in search of jobs that were not available. These children did not have a place to sleep and had nothing to eat.

There were thousands of children who did not have a home. The eastern cities built many orphanages during this period, but they were already filled with orphans.

The orphan train seemed to be a solution for these homeless children. They were put on a train and sent westward into the central part of the United States. This was a large, agricultural area that produced grains, vegetables, and meat animals.

The train would stop in Midwest cities and the children would line up in an open, flat train car. The public would inspect them and choose the ones they preferred. Sometimes, there were brothers and sisters. One would be chosen and the other would be left alone. Teenage boys and infants were chosen first. Older girls were chosen last. The boys were preferred to work on the farm. Infants adapted to a family culture.

Some orphans were privileged to get into a good family situation where they were treated with respect. Others were not so fortunate and lived a hard life of work and abuse.

4

JOHN RITTER
AND CHILDREN

Dear Grandma, John Ritter, Children

Dear Grandma Katie,
Several years later, you met a man named John Ritter. In June 1922, you and John got married, and your family moved to an area near Burnstadt, North Dakota. It was not fun for my mother and her siblings to leave the city of Ashley to move on a farm. My mother and her sisters used to reminisce about the times they were left alone on the farm when their parents would go visiting and to parties.

You and John had three more children:

Name	Birthdate
Elsie Ritter	May 15, 1922
George Ritter	April 3, 1927
Clarence Ritter	August 24, 1929

JOHN RITTER AND CHILDREN

Dear Grandma, Helen and Carrie

Dear Grandma Katie,

It was about this time when my mother, Helen, had to leave the family, because she was assaulted by her stepfather, John Ritter. She went to live with her grandparents in Ashley. That is where she went to school her last year and finished the seventh grade. She was thirteen.

Her sister, Carrie, went to her Uncle Johann Helfenstein Jr.'s family farm in the Coldwater area east of Ashley. She was twelve. Unfortunately, she had been assaulted by her Uncle John's oldest son.

Grandfather Johann Helfenstein Sr. reported these two violations to the law. Both men involved had to serve a term in prison. After John Ritter was released from prison, he came home to live with you, Grandma. Johann Helfenstein Sr., your father, was so angry with you because you took him back. He never forgave you and, as a result, he disowned you. I am so sorry because of all the hardships you endured in your life.

Dear Grandma, The Icehouse

Dear Grandma Katie,

My memories of you started when you lived in a little cottage in Wishek, North Dakota. It was a Sunday afternoon after lunch, and everyone was laying down to take a nap. My brother, LeRoy, was playing with your sons, George and Clarence. I was so bored and alone. Your little house had a nice yard.

The next place you moved was a finished basement and foundation. You planned to build a house on it. Our family visited you quite often on a Sunday afternoon.

My mother had a huge, white kettle about ten quarts in size. When she canned food, she used a hot water bath to seal jars. Grandma, you had a kettle just like my mother. I saw you cook white rice in that kettle many times. One day, when we came to your home, you said to my mother, "I cooked this rice, but I do not have any butter or lard to put on it."

My mother said, "I am so sorry. I wish we would have known because I have a lot of lard." I do not remember how they solved the problem.

What I remember most about your place was the icehouse you had in your backyard. It was a tall building lined with straw bales inside and out. The inside was filled with huge chunks of ice that was cut and brought from the river in the winter. My guess is that it was from the Missouri River.

In those days, people did not have refrigerators. They had iceboxes with good insulation. They would go to the icehouse and bring chunks of ice to put in their icebox which kept their food cool.

One day, a lady came to buy ice. You took a hammer and chisel and chopped off a piece. You asked her if it was the right size.

She said, "Yes. How much does it cost?"

You said, "Twenty-five cents."

Our First Family Car

As I remember, our first family car was a 1932 or 1933, loden green Whippet. It was a modern car in its time. It had four doors, and the wheels had wooden spokes.

One day, we took a trip to Aunt Carrie's house near Tappen, North Dakota. We only went there once a year. It was seventy miles from where we lived in the Venturia area, and the trip was long and tiring!

On our journey, we traveled twenty-five miles before we reached Wishek, then another twenty-five miles to Napoleon. We still had twenty more miles to go! We waited anxiously to see if we were going to stop for ice cream. We did stop there on one trip. Why couldn't we stop every time? It seemed like the older we got, the less our chances were of getting our favorite, frozen treat.

The roads were all gravel; the trip seemed endless. Each time the car stopped, my ears were ringing and hurting. I was glad when they went back to normal.

Another trip we took in the Whippet was to see Mother's Uncle John. It was only nine miles to Ashley and another seventeen miles east to Uncle John's farm. We were greeted by Aunt Margaret who was a sweet, little lady about forty years old. She didn't have any teeth, and her hair was pulled back in a bun. They had eight girls and two boys.

Our Whippet was also a luxury car. The windows had drawable curtains which could be open or shut. When the ignition key was removed, the doors and windows locked at the same time.

When our family went visiting relatives, the children would play outdoors. One time when I was only five, LeRoy began to bully and tease me. I became angry and fought back. He ran into the house and told Mother I was causing trouble. I remember, she put me in the Whippet and locked the doors. Some of the children were confused and some laughed.

Wintertime was always sad for the Whippet because my father took out the battery and put the wheels on blocks. Our transportation was the wagon and sleigh until spring.

Dear Grandma, I Should Have Written It Down

Dear Grandma Katie,

My mother told me this story about her wealthy aunt in California. Sometime after my mother and father were married, there was a notice that my mother was named in her aunt's will. There are questions I wish I would have asked. What year was this? Was I born then? If so, how old was I?

The story is so interesting because the letter which said that my mother was named in the will, said she needed to be present to receive her share of the trust. There was a lot of curiosity about the presentation.

My parents and my mother's grandparents took it upon themselves to drive to California. This may have taken place in the late 1920's and the roads to California were gravel. I don't know what kind of car they had then. I don't think they had the loden-green Whippet yet.

My parents had not been more than fifty miles out of the county in which they were born. They had never seen mountains! Father would have been the driver and had never been near a river! All he had ever seen was Hoskina Lake near Ashley, North Dakota. At this time, he had not even been to Bismarck, North Dakota.

Something came up. They changed their minds and did not plan to go. They could have sent my mother, Helen Esch Dockter, to California by train. However, being of German descent, she could not have represented herself. Those were the days when women were led to believe they could not think for themselves.

The aunt listed in the will had previously lost her arm in a car accident in California. As I remember, her maiden name was Augusta Helfenstein.

Dear Grandma, Edna

Dear Grandma Katie,

Your parents, Johann Sr. and Caroline Helfenstein, lived in Ashley, North Dakota. They took the train to Wishek to visit your house, and usually slept in Edna and Elsie's bedroom. At this time, my Aunt Edna was fourteen or fifteen years old.

On this particular night, Edna went out to a dance. As usual, she told her sister, Elsie, to leave the window open a crack so she could crawl in unnoticed after midnight.

Edna lifted one leg high into the window and stepped up to the bed in the bedroom. She landed right on top of your father and mother who were lying there sound asleep! They jumped up in surprise to see Edna on top of them. Needless to say, Edna was surprised too because she didn't know the grandparents were visiting that day!

The next morning, your parents were wondering where that poor child was that night because she had been locked out.

5

FLORENCE SCHOOLING

Crazy Pony Transportation

My father bought a Shetland pony and named her "Fern". She was petite and had a deep, reddish-brown mane and body. It didn't take us long to see that she was a nervous horse.

Father didn't talk much about his plans, but he was in the shop late one night. He had a large belt which may have been the drive belt of a threshing machine. He measured the horse and crafted a harness out of the old belt. After that, he built a cart the right size to fit the pony. It had a seat for two adults or three children. He was a man of six-foot stature. He had a brother, Emil, who was tall. After the harness and cart were ready, he invited his brother and they took Fern and the cart for a ride. She ran and ran for several miles. Her energy was endless. She did not stop running!

Fern was a restless pony and, perhaps, not the safest choice of transportation for young children.

Country School

My memories of school are not so exciting. I went to country school two miles from our home. It was a one-room school. Grades one through eight were all in one room. We were fortunate because our mother had a seventh-grade education and spoke both English and German Schwebich. We spoke both languages when we entered school.

We did not have a furnace in our home that provided heat for every room. When we awoke in the morning, our house was cold. Father built a fire in the parlor stove and in the cookstove in the kitchen. The water was frozen in the water pail. My shoes were cold when I put them on, and my overshoes were also cold.

After breakfast, my brother and I were ready to put on our cold coats and get on the cart that was hitched to our crazy pony, Fern. Off we went in a gallop going two miles into a below zero wind. I froze my feet many times — my little toe looked like a big, red plum. Many times, the schoolhouse was also cold when we arrived.

The first lesson we had was phonics. Our teacher was Mrs. Ursad. I can still see her standing in front of us with flashcards and pronouncing the letters and sounds. Phonics went on every day for weeks and the entire school was exposed to the lesson. If a student did not learn the first year, there was always a second year they were exposed to phonics. I do not remember any students not learning how to read well.

First grade transportation was another unforgettable event with Crazy Pony Fern and the two-wheel cart. I was seven and LeRoy was nine. Fern had to be held at the halter until she was hitched to the cart. The teacher usually held her at the halter and waited until I was on the cart and LeRoy had finished the hitching. He jumped on the cart holding the reins. Then Fern took a leap and ran two miles in full gallop and stopped short in front of the barn door at home.

One day, LeRoy hitched the cart to Fern, but could not get on the cart. Fern ran. I was on the cart without reins. She sped home and stopped in front of the barn door. Father had to drive Fern back to school to get LeRoy. Traveling to school with Fern was dangerous — but it was better than walking.

LeRoy's behavior was abusive in school — the same as it was at home. He would tease and bully me and hit my head with his fist. Our older cousins, Olive and Lorraine, got tired of his behavior and called him "a dumb a_hole". That shut him up.

Male Domination and German Background

I learned early in life that boys were stronger than girls. The male was the head of the household and made all the decisions. They were to conduct all business and deserved to be educated. They were also qualified to be witnesses in public affairs and marriage ceremonies.

My brother was two years older than I. From the time we received allowance, he received a dime and I got a nickel. If he got a nickel, I sometimes got a nickel too — but sometimes I got two pennies. When we went to the ice cream parlor, ice cream was five cents a cone. I was so happy when we each got a five-cent ice cream cone because my cone was just as large as my brother's! When my mother made homemade ice cream, she dished it out in little dishes. My brother's portion was always larger than mine. When we got apples or oranges, canned fruit, or candy, his portion was always larger.

If there was any sibling bickering, he was in control and pounded my head. I cried and Mother said to me, "It's your fault too." She allowed him to abuse us girls, my sister, Inez, and I. It never helped my migraine headaches.

Father never assaulted Mother or his daughters. When he was intoxicated, Mother warned me not to talk at dinner for fear that I might tell about LeRoy pounding my head.

The migraine headaches continued. I also got a temperature with the migraine. Later in life, my doctor pointed out to me that this was my body's way to attack the immune system. Mother never took me to the doctor. My headaches gradually became less frequent.

Leroy pounded my head in school one day. My cousin, Olive, was older than both Leroy and me. She said to Leroy, "Stop pounding Florence's head. I hate you."

Eventually, he quit because he was ashamed. I was also ashamed because I was the victim. Mother convinced me that it was my fault too.

Childhood Memories, Schooling

When I was a child, I never had a doll or toys. My father built a wooden doll bed for me. I remember I used to run back and forth from the shed to the house while he hand-crafted it. There were many little half-inch posts that were reinforced with a thin steel rod. These were the head and front sides. I don't know who painted it, I never got a doll that fit the bed.

Several years later when I was about seven, my mother and I were in a store. There were many dolls on display, she told me to pick one. When I did choose one, she thought there were nicer ones. So, she bought a brunette doll with a yellow, sheer dress. The eyes opened and closed, and it had porcelain face, arms and legs.

When we got home, I took the doll to my doll bed. It was about four inches longer than the bed! My mother took the doll and placed it in a corner close to the ceiling in the living room. The doll was there for years, until one day my mother was washing the walls. She gave the doll to my sister who was allowed to play with it. I don't know how that went. I do remember that I never had a doll. She told her friends that I did not have any interest in dolls.

As a child, I sensed that my mother always paid more attention to my brother, LeRoy, who was two years older than I. I do not remember her saying anything favorable to me or of me. She spent a lot of time with him. She would read to him and help him write his numbers and ABC's. There was no room for me on her lap – LeRoy was on her lap.

He was enrolled in the 1st grade at age five years and four months. He skipped 4th grade, and later was given the 7th grade state exams and passed them. He graduated from 8th grade at age eleven, and by age fifteen, he was a high school graduate.

Mother took me to school in September and I was six in October. She told the teacher that I couldn't learn. She compared me with LeRoy. The teacher told her to keep me at home because there would be two more 1st graders the next year. So, I was seven in the first grade. I had memorized most of the 1st grade readers from listening to my brother. My grades were always better than my classmates. But I started experiencing migraine headaches that year and missed a lot of school. After I was eight, my mother kept me out of school to babysit my four younger siblings.

Something happened in the 4th grade. Suddenly, my grades were below my classmates. I could not understand why my grades were dropping. When I wrote the 7th and 8th grade exams, I was a C- student. I was ashamed and embarrassed and put it all aside. It was many years after I was an adult that I realized my grades dropped because of all the days I missed school.

I was in charge of the household at fifteen. At that time, my sister, Inez, was ten and was playing with dolls. I was married at age seventeen, and LeRoy also got married. No one realized what an impact our marriages would have on the family. Inez had to help Mother with housekeeping and Father with farm work.

This was a rude awakening for her at age twelve. Many years later, she told me they missed me. There was a void in the family structure which no one was aware of until I was gone. The family had to restructure all the chores I had done. My mother cried a lot.

I lived fifty miles from the home where I grew up, and the only transportation was by car. The roads were gravel-topped, and cars could only travel about 35 to 40 mph. At that time, there were no rural telephones.

I was so busy doing farm work, I do not remember being homesick. After my marriage, in fact, I worked much harder than when I lived at home.

Confirmation Day

This was a sad day for me because I felt I had missed out on a spiritual part of life. The Heidelberg catechism was in high German, a language I did not understand. Because it was a mystery, the day was a total blank to me.

I did not understand high German. My mother did not bother to help me learn the language. The sermon at my wedding was the first English sermon I ever heard in my church.

The first part of the confirmation took place in the morning service which was attended by the congregation. The second half was held in the afternoon. Our family went home for lunch.

While we were eating our lunch, Father said to me, "It seems to me you were the prettiest girl in the confirmation class."

Mother disagreed with him. This was a very unusual comment from my father. Perhaps, he sensed the sadness in me.

Recovering From Shame and Rejection

I don't remember sitting on my mother's lap. My brother, LeRoy, was two years older than I. They were always doing something when LeRoy was sitting on Mother's lap. I must have been very small because I vaguely remember my brother having crayons and drawing numbers and letters, or reading a book. There was no room for me on Mother's lap.

Sometimes, I was so bored. There were no books or toys in our house. I never had a doll. The only thing I could find was the Sears mail order catalog. I would look at the toys and little girls' dresses.

I don't remember my mother calling me "Florence." She addressed my brother, LeRoy, by his name.

There aren't many photos of me when I was growing up. I had to have permission from my mother to be on a picture with my younger siblings.

Many times, my mother told my sisters, Inez and Gladys, to get ready to go to Ashley to shop. I was always left at home to do the dishes or other chores.

6

CHILDHOOD
RESPONSIBILITES

Self-Sufficiency

We were fortunate that Father had a farm. We did not have any money at the time, but we always had a place to live. We had meat and potatoes and a garden. Mother did a lot of canning: fifty quarts each of corn, green beans, beets, sauerkraut, vegetable mix for soup, pickles, and tomatoes. Don't forget the peas which I had to pick in the morning and shell in the afternoon – and at the same time keep an eye on my younger siblings. My mother was working in the field or in town. That was a lot to expect of a nine-year-old. After I was married, I said, "No more peas for me!"

Cleaning Mother's House

Did Mother know she was training me to clean her house when I was five years old? I remember the dust rag. It looked dirty and oily. It smelled strong and burned my nose. She told me all the furniture in the living room had to be dusted and cleaned. If it was not clean, I had to do it over. The traditional German background I came from believed, "Cleanliness is next to godliness."

When I was about ten years old, all the housecleaning had to be done on Saturday. It was our cleaning day — getting ready for Sunday, the day of rest. My first chore was washing the breakfast dishes. Next, I changed all the bedding, mopped the floors, and dusted the furniture. By then, it was time to prepare lunch. After the lunch dishes were cleaned, I started to clean the kitchen cupboards, the stove (inside and out), and washed the wooden kitchen chairs. Everything had to be cleaned in the kitchen except the floor. The next project was baking pie or other desserts. Last, was scrubbing and waxing the kitchen floor. Sometimes, Mother allowed me to wash my hair and put it in curlers. If my hair in the curlers was not dry, I had to wear a scarf to cover them to go to town on Saturday night. My friends had ribbons in their hair. I had curlers in mine.

Sunday was a day of misery for me. We went to a church service in the little church on the hill ¼ of a mile from our farm. The church service was one hour of Sunday School for youth and children and one hour for singing and worship. This two-hour service was in high German, a language which most children did not understand. After we came home from church, we had lunch which was mostly prepared on Saturday. It consisted of noodle soup, potato salad, some meat, and pie. We were not allowed to use the scissors on Sunday. This eliminated all crafts.

I overheard my mother telling her friends several times, she was waiting for me to finish the eighth grade so she could make life easy for herself! I knew there was no plan for me to go to high school because I was a girl.

Scrubbing the Kitchen Floor

My father inherited a one-bedroom bungalow on the farm from Grandfather Dockter Jr. When my parents moved in, they put on an addition. The house became a wing type, L-shaped home. It had one bedroom, a living room, and a kitchen with an entry.

I do not remember the first floor covering in the kitchen, but I do remember the one that was installed when I was ten. Mother was pregnant with Gladys. It was white with an inlaid design of small black and red blocks. The design went into the base of the flooring and never wore out. The surface was porous like cement.

My mother showed me how to clean it. I had to use Bon-Ami (Ajax) to scrub the surface, then rinse it with clear water. After it dried, the last process was to apply a coat of wax. This was a weekly job and I did it for five years. My hands were chapped and bloodied, and my knees were sore. I have never forgotten that floor covering.

Dear Grandma, I Created Running Water

Dear Grandma Katie,

During my childhood, the well on our farm was 130 feet deep and about thirty yards from the house. A tower and the windmill were on top of the well. When the wind was blowing, it was easy to draw water. One day, my mother sent my brother and me to get some water. However, on that day, there was no wind and we had to use the pump handle. This was difficult. It took both of us to get 1/2 a pail of water. I think he was eight years old and I was six.

It was about that same time when my mother gave me 1/2-gallon jelly bucket to carry water into the house. That day was windy, and the windmill was running. That was the day I started running water for our family.

Soon, I was running water with a gallon bucket. After that, it was a three-gallon water pail made of white porcelain. It had a dipper and everybody in the house drank from it. The whole household used this water and it seemed empty all the time! Later, I also ran water with the pail for bath time.

I ran water with the pail for my family for many years. It seemed I was always running for water and carrying dirty water out of the house.

Annual Meat Preparation

I cried many days because I could not go to grade school. Some days my parents did not send me to school. There were times I missed three or four days with migraine headaches. My parents believed that it was a waste of time to send a girl to school because she could learn how to keep house and wash diapers while she was in the family home.

I had to stay home from school when my mother washed clothes. I had to hold and care for the baby. I stayed home from school when my mother went shopping. There were no heaters in the car and sometimes my parents went to town with a wagon or sleigh hitched to the horses. I had to stay home from school and take care of the kids. I also stayed home from school when my parents did the butchering in October.

Our annual meat preparation took place in October. My parents usually butchered three or four hogs. It was not a pleasant chore. Sometimes I tried to be busy somewhere else. The hog killing was done by Father and his brother, Emil. The process was to shoot the hog in the head. After it quit struggling, they would stab the heart and bleed the hog.

Early in the morning of the first day, my parents placed two boilers on the cookstove which were filled with water from the well. When the water was brought to the boiling point, they brought it out of the house and took it to the barn. It was poured into a 50-gallon wood barrel which my father carefully put under a manger. It was tilted to a degree so the hog could be immersed and scalded. Each hog was scraped, and the hair was singed clean. The next step was to gut the inside and clean the organs such as the heart, liver, and kidneys. They removed the brains which became a cooked delicacy. Our father was fond of them, and I learned to like the flavor too. Then the hogs were strung up and left in the barn to cool overnight.

On the second day, the hogs were dismembered. The hind legs were cured for ham. All the other pork was cut and ground in a hand grinder. It was an all-day job. At the end of a long day, the ground pork was hand mixed and seasoned to our family's taste. The seasoning was a mixture of salt, pepper, and lots of garlic. Mother shelled, peeled, and mashed about a cup of garlic which was steeped in hot water and put through a strainer. All went into the sausage mixture. This work was done by my parents and Aunt Albina and Uncle Emil in the basement.

After the sausage was mixed, the next step was to run it through the sausage stuffer. This was a gallon size, cast iron container with a lid which compressed by turning a handle which made the sausage. I was upstairs taking care of my younger siblings, cooking meals, and helping by bringing water in from the well and carrying the wastewater out.

On the third day, Father did the chores. After that, he prepared brine to cure the ham. He filled a 20-gallon crock about half-full of water and added enough salt until an egg would swim. After stirring it, he put the ham in the crock and let it cure for several days until the meat was cured to the bone.

While working with the ham, he had built a wood fire in the smokehouse which gave off a great aroma! Later, the racks of iron inside held 200 pounds of wonderful, smoked sausage!

The smokehouse was made of 30-gallon barrels which were split and flattened to make a round metal building. It was 6 feet in diameter and about 8 feet tall with a metal chimney at the top. It had a metal door with a lock on it. Overall, it was a piece of art and beauty! Very innovative!

We had smoked sausage until spring. Mother canned some sausage in half gallon jars. It was a real treat to enjoy in the summer months.

After the ham was properly cured, Father also smoked the ham in the smokehouse. That process took several days.

While Father was working with the sausage and ham, the pork rinds were rendered into lard. Mother and I ground the pork skins and trimmed pork fat in preparation for making lye soap. The lard was put into a 4-gallon crock. This had white and blue rims around the outside. It was given to her by some of her ancestors. Lard was essential in every kitchen that survived the Dustbowl and Financial Crash days.

Day four of the butchering process involved canning liver sausage and head cheese. Those two sausages were always canned and stored in the cellar for use after the red meat was all gone. Those were days I should have been in school.

There was always a big mess to be cleaned up after the butchering. I was lucky if I could go to school on day five!

The last chore was to combine pork rinds, lard and drippings, and about eight cans of lye. The acid in the lye made the mixture hot. This recipe could make the best and most powerful soap. Mother used two wooden peach fruit boxes and lined each box with a layer of cotton fabric. After the lye soap was mixed and stirred to the correct consistency, it was poured into the boxes and allowed to cool and set. After 24 hours, it could be cut into soap bars. It was the only laundry soap we ever used at the time.

In addition to pork, we butchered one beef animal, several geese, Rowan ducks, and many year-old laying hens. Mother usually sold about forty laying hens each year. It was a fun day to sell the hens that we brought to Ashley in cages. They were worth about $1 each. Mother would use the money to buy school supplies and other things that were needed in the household.

About two years after World War II, the demand for food came down. The government did not have to support a large military force. The price for farm commodities dropped drastically. When Mother brought the laying hens to the market, the buyer said the hens had no value at all. Mother and I butchered and canned all those hens. We had noodle soup and chicken all year. It was a sad day the day we had to take the hens home and butcher them.

7

INEZ

The Sheep Buck Saw Me

Dear Grandma Katie,

My sister, Inez, was born when I was four and a half years old. The morning after she was born, my Aunt Philipena was staying at our house. She was a short, stout lady who was very kind and loving. She always wore her rayon, crêpe, black dress to church. When she went out on casual days, she sometimes wore a cotton dress, or she had an apron over her best black dress.

That morning, she gave me a bucket and sent me to the back shed to get fresh milk for breakfast. It was a stormy, Wednesday morning and my father was in the shed separating milk. When I got close to the shed, I noticed the doors were closed. There was a sheep buck nearby, but he was looking toward the water tank and did not see me.

Father did not know I was trying to get into the shed, but he did hear the noise I made! When the sheep buck turned and saw me, he quickly charged and rolled me over several times. My screams got my father's attention. The milk bucket was gone, but I still had my all-day sucker in my left hand! It was a yellow, corncob sucker with green husks and was now covered in sheep wool. My Aunt Philipena cleaned me up, washed all my bruises, and washed the wool off my all-day sucker. It was good as ever!

Dear Grandma, Inez Recovers, Local Stores and Mom's Hand-tooled Purse

Dear Grandma Katie,

It was winter when my little sister, Inez, became ill with the croup which is like bronchitis. She was only two or three months old and had a high temperature with a deep, chest cough. It was the third time she had been so sick! Most people did not bother to go to the doctor because there was no form of treatment at the time. It was before penicillin became available to the public. The only thing they could do was use home remedies and bed rest.

Charles and Irene Johnstone owned the country store in Venturia, North Dakota. They were English and came from the East. They may have been Swedish, Norwegian, or another nationality. Our local community was solid Germans from Russia, so anyone who did not speak that language was considered English from the East. Irene Johnstone had some knowledge of health remedies. My father went to town two miles away and brought Irene to our home to treat the baby and make her comfortable.

Irene instructed my mother to prepare a hot jacket by taking a kimono and lining it with a cotton batting. Meanwhile, Irene cooked a mustard plaster. I didn't know what the formula was. It seemed onions and mustard were the main ingredients. The stench was strong and horrible! It burned my nose and eyes. What a relief it was to see her take it off the stove! The next step was to put the mustard plaster on the baby's chest, put the hot jacket on her, and wrap her in warm blankets. It looked like they wanted to cook the baby.

Irene was a very compassionate, sincere person. She told my parents that the baby was very ill, and that the treatment she had given should help the fever break by midnight. "If the fever does not break by then," she said, "we are in serious trouble." Mother and Father sat by the baby's bed and watched to see what her reaction would be. The fever did break by midnight.

Charles and Irene's store was a pleasant place to be. It was a long building with a counter on each side the full length of the store. Behind the counter, all the merchandise was stacked neatly on shelves. They had everything that was needed for a household, except hardware. The long, center aisle had chairs and benches for mothers to rest, hold their babies, and visit. It provided the best social time for many country women, and it was where we could find our mothers after they had sold the eggs to the Johnstone store and purchased groceries.

Most of the time, our mother had a few pennies, nickels, or sometimes dimes left for our allowance. She had a hand tooled, leather purse about six inches wide and five inches deep. It had a narrow handle and a clasp as wide as the purse at the top. It may have been the only handbag she ever had up to that time. She would open the clasp with her hand, leave the purse open, and reach for the little coin purse. She would give me a penny, nickel, or a dime. Usually it was a nickel. Sometimes, she only had a penny for me. I never questioned what the reason was for the coin I got.

Then it was time for me to decide what to buy. Irene and Charles had a son that was in business with them. He went by the name of A.Z. I'm not sure the reason he had for that, but I always waited for A.Z. to complete my purchase. In the candy section there was a row of candy boxes. There were chocolate clusters, chocolate covered peanuts, jellybeans, candied cherries, coconut bons, Boston peanuts, orange slices, lemon drops — an endless selection! There was a choice of bag size in which to put the candy. For five cents, A.Z. would sell me a brown bag about five inches tall filled with chocolate covered peanuts.

The next step was the hardware store, to see who was there, or perhaps mail a letter. The store was owned by the Weidman brothers. John was a kind and gentle man. Philip was short tempered and hotheaded. Sometimes I had to mail a letter. I always waited my turn to buy a three-cent stamp from John — hoping not to get close to Phillip!

The Little Town of Venturia

My family farm was two miles north of Venturia. At the time, the population was approximately 300. We did not have any outing experience apart from school, church, and relatives. The town of Venturia was our greatest delight!

Our entire community went to town on Tuesday and Saturday nights to sell their farm products. The eggs were sold at the grocery store and the cream was sold at the cream buyer's store.

My duty at the time was to do the same as I did at home. I had to take care of my younger siblings until my mother completed her shopping. I felt sorry for myself because my friends had a good time running up and down the wooden sidewalks of Venturia. But I always got in on some of the fun!

The wooden sidewalks sometimes gave us trouble because every time we dropped a coin, it went into one of the spaces and was gone. Dropping a penny was bad, but not as bad as dimes. The coins we got were usually what Mother had left after the grocery bill. She was pretty good at balancing the bill, so there was money left for our allowances. Sometimes it was a dime or a nickel. If we were lucky, she had an extra penny for each of us!

The Community Band of Venturia was the delight of the town. It was the only source of entertainment in the area. Originally, it was composed of men and boys from the farm community, but had to break up during World War II. After the war, the band was reorganized. It consisted of girls and boys of the community and some married persons.

The band performed on the grandstand in the summertime. On Tuesday nights, people from neighboring communities would also enthusiastically appear to enjoy our Straus waltzes and other melodies. I was in the clarinet section, and was later chosen as drum majorette. My sister, Inez, played a French horn. It was a blessing for me and my sister. It was the only organization we could be in, and we learned to read music.

My Most Embarrassing Moment

It was a hot, Sunday afternoon in July, and I was home alone. My cousin, Violet, came to our house suggesting we go to the Bertsch Dam for a swim. She was seventeen, and I was fourteen. She was driving her family car, a light green Nash.

"Just wear your swimsuit," she said. "We'll go for a dip and come back soon."

It sounded like fun to me.

We had to go through Venturia to get to the dam. When we got there, we took a spin around town to see what was going on. Before long, we saw black smoke coming from under the hood! Her Nash stopped.

Several people emerged from their houses to see the event. Some older men quickly put out the fire on the motor, and a kind gentleman carefully repaired the wiring. In the meantime, Violet and I stood there in our bathing suits! These were the days when women could not even be seen in shorts. It seemed like forever until we could leave, and we went home. I didn't tell my parents about our dilemma.

On Monday morning, my father always went to town. When he came home at lunchtime, he had heard the whole story. After roasting me, he said, "It was not nice."

However, we found out the fire was a blessing in disguise. We were told that the Bertsch Dam was man-made, and we didn't know where the drop-off was. Neither of us could swim, and no one would have known what happened to us that day until they found us.

It was good we did not go to the dam!

My First Flower Garden

My love for flowers came early in life. I was about ten years old and had always wished for a flower garden of my own. I chose a place beside the house next to a tall, lilac bush. The soil looked like clay and was hard. Maybe, it had never been tilled. It was difficult work to spade and make a seed bed in that poor soil. I decided cow manure would also soften it up. After it was spread, I spaded the soil once more. I do not recall how

I got the manure from the barnyard to the side of the house, but I must have carried it in pails.

After raking the soil even, I was ready to plant the flower seeds Mother had purchased. I planned that the back row would be the tall cosmos. It grew about four feet tall and the blossoms were from white and pink to dark burgundy. In front of them would be the zinnias. These were multi-color white, pink, yellow, orange, and burgundy and grew to about three feet. The third row would be the four o'clocks. These were white and red and only bloomed until the sun was bright! They grew to be two feet tall. The fourth row would be the lovely marigolds. These were yellow and burgundy and stood twelve inches tall. These were all hardy flowers. They did not need much water and produced seed which could be harvested and then planted the next year.

When I got up every morning, I went to see if there were flower seeds breaking the ground. It seemed forever until there were any plants. At last, there were rows of flower plants!

There were many surprises in my flower garden project. Rover, our farm dog, liked the soft soil. On a hot day, it was a cool place for him to lay! Also, when our chickens found the flower bed, they enjoyed nesting in the cool soil and fluffing their feathers. I spent hours patrolling and guarding my flower garden!

Eventually, the flowers were in full bloom. My father could then see the beauty of the flowers. He could also see the determination in me — and my frustration. The hens did not stop nesting in the flower bed. They were cleaning their feathers.

When Father came home from town that day, he surprised me. He brought a roll of chicken netting and some steel posts to put a fence around my flower garden. That was the time I could enjoy my flower garden.

The Attic In Our Two-Room House

Our two-room farmhouse was built by my father's uncle, Gust Dockter. He and his wife did not have any children. It had nice, hardwood floors. The large room served as the bedroom and living room. The small room was the kitchen with a cooking stove, cupboards, and a table. In the winter, a cream separator was also in the kitchen. I didn't like the smell of the separator because it had a pan in the bottom to collect oil and overflow. The smell was awful.

My parents bought an addition to the house when I was four and my brother was six. While the building was going on, we were always warned not to step on boards with nails. I did step on a nail. It was very painful, and it took a long time to heal.

There was an outside set of stairs which led to the attic. My mother had many things in storage and did not want us to go up there. However, it was an interesting experience for us to look at what we could find: the clothes we outgrew, the Christmas goodies she bought as she could afford them, and the Christmas tree. It was in a box in the attic. It was about 24 inches tall and the branches were folded close to the trunk of the tree. We unfolded the branches, set it up, and put on the decoration bulbs and clips that held the candles. We also tried to put on the tinsel that had been used for many years. On Christmas Eve, we lit the candles and watched them burn until they all melted down. It was then that we got the Christmas candy and nuts that Mother had carefully hidden in our attic.

More Confusion, Passing On Shame

One Sunday afternoon, we had company. This was always a happy event when mother's sisters visited us. Uncle Ben and Aunt Carrie, their son, Virgil, Aunt Edna and her new husband, Stan Crossaint.

The men and boys always found something interesting in the farmyard. They were looking at our crazy horse, Fern. Even though Stan was six feet tall, he could see no reason why he could not ride this little, Shetland pony. He got on the pony, but he did not have control of her. The pony went straight for the clothesline and Stan got caught by the line on his neck! It was not pleasant for him and when he walked away, there was a lot of laughter. The ladies watched this comedy from the kitchen window.

We lived in a small house and I did not have a doll, toys, or books. I was there to do some chores that my mother wanted me to do. Since there was only a highchair or cradle to put the baby in, I was holding the baby. I was in the kitchen enjoying listening to my mother and aunts.

During the conversation, Aunt Edna told us that she and her husband were expecting a baby. My mother gave me a stern, awful look. The first chance she had after her sisters left, she told me how awful I was to sit and listen to my aunt tell about the coming baby. She said I should have excused myself and left the room. I do not remember how old I was then. After being exposed to and taking care of my siblings my entire life, I knew were babies came from and why they came. This was another way of my mother "passing on shame."

Dear Grandma, Letter One

Dear Grandma Katie,

Grandma, I enjoyed the letters that you wrote to me when I was about eight years old. I do not remember much about what you wrote. I am so sorry I did not keep any of those lovely letters. I do remember that you always closed the letter signed, "Love you, Your Grandma XXXXX."

I have wondered many times what you were trying to tell me. I am sure that you could see what my mother was doing to me. You used to travel with your son, Andrew. He drove a *Stucker* truck. He stopped at your home in Wishek, North Dakota, and picked you up and brought you to our farm near Venturia. I was always excited to see you come.

One time, you came in the fall. I was about ten years old then. The next morning after chores and breakfast, my mother told me to wash the cream separator, make all the beds, dust mop all the rooms, and wash the dishes after my siblings had finished breakfast. My mother told me that both of you would go to the garden and pick tomatoes because there was a frost warning that night. My mother knew that picking the tomatoes was the highlight of the year for me. After I had done all my assigned chores and you and Mother had picked the tomatoes, it was lunch time. After lunch, our Uncle Andy stopped and picked you up and took you home to Wishek.

That afternoon, my mother and I took the tomatoes up to the attic. We noticed the tomatoes were wet because there was heavy dew that morning. The tomatoes were not ripe at that stage and the dew caused dark spots before they were ripe to be canned. Most of them spoiled. I never got to be with you that day.

One day, Uncle Andy surprised us. He stopped at our farm and left his wife, Wilma, at our place. I was at school. When I came home, Wilma said, "Who is this girl?"

My mother said, "It is Florence."

Aunt Wilma was in awe. She said to me, "You are so tall. You are a young lady and, oh, so beautiful!"

My mother stepped in and said, "Look at Florence's big nose. Just look at it." My mother meant what she said.

8

SIBLING DEATH - FLORENCE PEARL, STANLEY JULIUS

Florence Pearl, Stanley Julius, and Gladys

My sister, Florence Pearl, was born in 1927 in our two-room farmhouse. The first year of her life was like that of a normal one-year-old. She carefully learned how to walk. Mother noticed that though she was growing, her tummy was out of proportion with the rest of her body. Her tummy seemed to get larger in a short time. After a while, she would lose her balance. Eventually, she could no longer walk.

My parents took her to Dr. Curtiss. After examining her, he walked to the window of his office and stood there for a while, gazing into a blank scene. He turned around and walked back to my parents and the baby. He had a painful, sad look on his face. He knew what the diagnosis was. The disease was Wilms' disease, a cancerous tumor on the kidney. He also knew the cure was removal of the kidney and tumor. The problem here was, there were tumors on both kidneys. The doctor's advice was to go to Mayo Clinic.

At the time, my mother was nineteen and my father, Julius, was twenty-two. They also knew that there was another child on the way. Going to Rochester, Minnesota, was a mystery to them. Neither of them had been outside the state of North Dakota, except to Eureka, South Dakota. Arrangements were made for my mother and her sister, Carrie, to take Florence Pearl to Mayo Clinic. My guess is that Grandfather Gottlieb Jr. took over the travel and any other arrangements that were needed. He had great faith in doctors. He had many experiences and knowledge from the time his wife, Christine Villhauer, became ill and died. My father stayed at home to take care of the farm.

Mother and her sister enjoyed each other's company very much. The train trip to Minnesota would have been very exciting, but not under these circumstances. When they arrived at the clinic, they soon realized that Dr. Curtiss' diagnosis was correct. They were told that removal of the tumors was not a possibility because both kidneys could not be removed. The Mayo doctors gave her approximately six months to live. She died when she was one year and eight months old.

Two months after she died, my brother, LeRoy, was born. This was June 1929. I was born in October 1931. Inez was born in June 1936. Then another brother, Stanley Julius, was born in July 1938. I was six years old. Stanley seemed to be a special delight. He had large, brown eyes. All of us had blue eyes like our father. Stanley had brown eyes like our mother. He was a beautiful, healthy, active, large baby as all in our family were.

Living in a small house with three rooms, there was not much privacy. My mother would usually put a blanket on the kitchen table, and sponge bathe the baby every day. One Sunday morning while she was getting ready to go to church, she bathed Stanley and massaged his body. He was about nine months old at the time. She would guide her thumbs on his rib cage and pull up four fingers from the spine to the tummy. It was while her hands came up to the tummy, that she stopped short. A bewildered look of horror stood still on her face. She was spellbound as if she did not want to move anymore. As the tears began to gather in her eyes, she kept running her fingers over the area on one side of his waist. He was uncomfortable while she did this, and squirmed and cried. In the meantime, my father came into the room. Mother said, "Put your hand on the baby's back and side, and feel this hard lump."

Father felt the area with his hand and his answer was, "He must be constipated." Though he was trying to console her, she was rather insulted by the suggestion. By then, the family was in turmoil with going to doctors. The diagnosis was Wilms' disease, the same as my sister's. There was a lot of assurance because there was only one kidney involved. They considered this curable because when they removed one kidney, Stanley could still function well with the remaining one.

By this time, Stanley had learned to walk and was scheduled for surgery at St. Alexis Hospital in Bismarck, North Dakota. We did not have telephone service at that time. Arrangements were very difficult without good communication. My parents were informed they would need to have two persons present for a possible blood transfusion. My father could not leave the farm at the time. My brother was two years older than I, but was not a candidate for transfusion because he had hay fever and allergies. My parents thought his blood was not good. And so, I was the most logical person for transfusion. I was seven years old and maybe weighed sixty pounds.

My mother, the baby Stanley, and I traveled to Bismarck to prepare for the surgery. I counted the days and hours before going there because I thought they were going to take all my blood. Because we did not have any money to go to a hotel, we stayed at my mother's cousin's place. Cousin Margaret's family had seven or eight children. We stayed a couple of days while the hospital was preparing little Stanley for his surgery.

It was horrible when we checked him at the hospital that day. He was only one year old, and screamed when we had to leave the hospital. I don't know which was worse: watching him scream or me thinking about the time they were going to take all my blood. We were not allowed to visit him. We were allowed to observe him, but could not let him see us.

The surgery was delayed a week because he had eczema that needed to be treated. We were scheduled to be at the hospital a few days before the surgery for blood tests to see if my mother or I were a match for his blood. My mother and I were waiting in the room for the nurse. The door opened and a beautiful, fair skinned, blue-eyed, slender nun came in. She addressed my mother and sympathized with her for the surgery her baby was to have. She said, "We have you down here for a blood donor, and when will this Florence Dockter be here?"

My mother said, "This is she sitting beside me."

The nurse put her arm around me and said, "This little girl can't give blood. I doubt if she has enough for herself." I don't remember how the blood situation turned out. All I know is, they didn't take all my blood.

The surgery was a success. The tumor was the size of a quart jar. After the surgery, my mother and I went 100 miles back to Venturia. My mother returned two weeks later to visit little Stanley. He did not recognize his mother anymore, but he raised up his arms when the nurses came in to care for him. To my mother, it was though a part of him had died. He had been hospitalized approximately one month, and had to learn to walk again.

Our family rejoiced over the success of the surgery and that our little, brown-eyed Stanley would be with us always. He became a strong toddler and very active. It was my job to babysit him, try to change him, clean him up, and keep him out of trouble. I enjoyed fussing with his hair. I put metal curlers in his hair which he hated. When it was dry, I would take the curlers out, take him to the mirror, and say, "How pretty you are!" I always had a special place in my heart for him because I knew how close he was to death at one time.

Everything went well until he turned two. He had his birthday in July and seemed fine until late summer and fall. In October and November, he began to have frequent colds and a cough. These became more intense, and eventually the symptoms were like pneumonia. Since there were no antibiotics at the time, these symptoms were a real concern.

My parents took him to Ashley to Dr. Mercklein who delivered me and my younger siblings. Knowing the history of little Stanley and the Wilms' disease, he suggested a lung biopsy. When the report came back, the doctor informed my parents there was a tumor in Stanley's lung. He needed to find out if it was benign or cancerous. The test was sent to Bismarck, and the results came back that it was cancerous.

Dr. Mercklein arranged an appointment for them to take Stanley to the clinic in Bismarck. By then, it was winter and close to Christmas. I can't remember how they took him to Bismarck. The trauma was so confusing sometimes, that it didn't matter what would happen next. I do know when they brought him home, they knew he was terminally ill. It was only a matter of time until his passing.

That evening was dull and gray as we sat around the dim, kerosene light, and tried to eat our simple dinner. While this was going on, we really had only a depressed mother and an addicted father. I wonder many times how much he remembered of all that had passed.

It was a long time of waiting. It was a very depressing winter to know that our little brother was going to die. I had turned nine in October.

Even though we were so poor at the time, we always had a hired girl. She stayed with us during the time Stanley was terminal, and helped take care of him.

It was February when I sensed that my mother was pregnant. When I came home from school, my mother and Stanley were usually in the bedroom. They spent most of their time in the bed the last six to eight weeks. Mother was trying to keep Stanley comfortable. Because of his lack of oxygen, he always wanted to lean on her. Breathing was easier for him in a half sitting position, but it made Mother very uncomfortable in her stage of pregnancy. Our country school usually was over by March 30.

April 18, 1941, was a cold, rainy, dreary day. Ella, the girl who was with us, was keeping us quiet in the kitchen. My mother came into the kitchen and said to Ella, "He is expiring." Then, I knew he had died.

Ella told LeRoy to go to the field and summon Father. After a while, Father came home with the horses. LeRoy was eleven. He took the horses, unhitched them, and put them in the barn.

In the meantime, Father came into the house. Mother was standing, leaning on the windowsill, and crying out loud. Father walked up to her, touched her, and said, "He is God's child, and we have to give him up. He is not ours any longer."

He went to the bedroom, took his son's body, and brought him out. He laid him on the kitchen table which had a blanket on it. From there, he went to call our neighbor lady, Sophia Haas, who came to prepare Stanley's body. Father excused himself to go to Ashley to get a coffin. He had hitched the two-wheeled trailer to the Model A Ford car to bring it home.

Meanwhile, Sophia was taking Stanley's clothes off and giving him a sponge bath. Sophia was a kind, Christian lady. She told my mother not to touch Stanley if it bothered her because she was in the last stages of pregnancy. She reminded my mother of the child she was carrying.

My mother went to the bedroom and came out with two new sets of clothes. They were called "romper sets". One was ivory and heather maroon. The other was off-white and royal blue. Sophia said they were both beautiful. Mother said to me, "Which should we put on him?"

I said, "The white and blue."

It took so terribly long for Father to bring the coffin. Stanley was still laying in the kitchen table, and it was getting dark. Mother told Ella, LeRoy, and me to go out and do the chores. We finished doing chores. I don't know if LeRoy took the harnesses off the horses.

When Father came home with the coffin, he said the delay was that it had cost $35. I don't know if they had an undertaker in Ashley at that time. The furniture store carried coffins as part of their business. Whoever sold it to him, sent him to welfare first for the $35 compensation.

Father brought the coffin into our unheated, entrance room next to the kitchen. He picked up Stanley Julius's body, carried it out to the entrance, and gently put it in. The lighting was dim – perhaps a lantern. I could not see it very well that night.

The next day, my parents opened the coffin to see how well the body was laid. He had a peaceful look on his face. Some of the puffiness of his face was gone. This had been due to lack of oxygen and kidney failure.

The three days he was lying in state seemed forever. There were no electric lights. Many times, I was told to go out there and get something from the pantry. It was a nightmare for me to go there when the coffin was there.

The funeral was in the little country church. When we got there, the little, white coffin was in front of the altar. It was covered with white velvet damask, and the interior was a pure white, satin fabric. Mother and Father sat on two wooden chairs in front of the coffin. I can't remember where I sat or who sat with me. All I could see was Father and Mother on those two chairs. Mother wore a chalice, navy blue, polka dot maternity dress. Her hair was grown out with no perm. I could not understand the songs or the sermon.

The funeral was so sad. There was so much sympathy for my parents and for the hardships that our family had experienced. Aunt Leah's and Ella's husbands, Ted and Arthur, sat in the car. They were sad, and did not go in the church.

It was a sorrowful and upsetting day. I did not know about the love of God, or the saving grace of Jesus Christ. The only wish I had was that we could someday meet little Stanley Julius in heaven. The next day after the funeral, Mother spent the afternoon walking in the yard, crying out loud. At noon, Father came home from the field, intoxicated as usual. Mother did not realize that Father was also grieving his son, Stanley Julius.

And so, the next ten days went — until May 2 when my sister, Gladys, was born. Later in life, Father told me about Mother in labor. When the time came for her to bear down, her labor quit. Dr. Mercklein said, "She has given up on life." The doctor gave her an injection to start labor again, and the birth took place.

Our mother did not have much interest in Gladys. She did not have time to grieve her 2½ year old son.

Mother breast-fed the baby. However, after Gladys was a few weeks old, Mother trained me to bathe and diaper her, hold her, and keep her comfortable. I was nine years old. That was my job until school started.

I could not understand why my mother would say, "Why don't you pick Gladys up? She has been waiting for you to come home from school?" I knew she could not sit by herself by then. I did not realize that I had been mothering my little sister.

While all these tragedies were upon our family, our mother took all the grieving upon herself. She did not realize that our father was suffering from the disease of alcoholism. His behavior caused her to be angry. She did not know that he was a sick person.

Gladys was a quiet, beautiful baby who did not require any attention. I don't remember her needing anything. She never got into trouble. But when she was six and started school, she seemed to go through a personality change. It was so cute. She started to say, "No! No!" I had never heard her say, "No" before. However, she was still the same quiet, poised, soul that she is today.

Dear Grandma, Six Months After The First Stanley Died

Dear Grandma Katie,

When I got ready to go to school one morning, my mother said I could not go because she and Father were going to a funeral in our church. It was a small church with fifty members located beside State Highway 11, 1/4 mile from our farm. I started to cry. She said I had to take care of my sister, Gladys, who was about six months old.

When it was time for my parents to go to the funeral, Mother said she changed her mind. She was not going. I started to cry again because it was too late for me to go to school.

Then she said to me, "You can go to the funeral with Father."

The funeral was for a stillborn, baby boy. It was the Adam Rudolph's family. Their four, school-age girls were not present, as I remember. When I walked into the church, the first thing I saw was a small, white brocade coffin which was exactly like that of my 2½ year old brother, Stanley, who had passed away six months before. There were no other children in church that day. I was ten years old. I sat beside one of the ladies who was an aunt of the stillborn baby.

I was in shock. My tears started to roll down my face. One of the church ladies asked me if I was not feeling well. Another lady asked if I wanted to go outside. My tears would not stop. My grieving was greater than the day my little brother died.

My father was seated on the right side with the other men. I don't know if he saw what was going on with me that day. It was never brought up. Did it go by unnoticed?

Dear Grandma, Memories of Stanley Julius

Dear Grandma Katie,

After he had recovered from his major surgery, Stanley Julius was about twenty months old. He was active and tall for his age.

Our family went to Venturia on Saturday and Tuesday nights to shop as usual. My mother said I would have to take care of the kids while she was getting the groceries. She also usually sat on the visiting bench and talked with her friends.

While she was visiting, Stanley would try to get into the cookie boxes and anything that was in his reach. So, I would pick him up and carry him. I was about nine at the time. One of the ladies from the area would watch me carry Stanley, and always said to me, "That child is too heavy for you." Her name was Mrs. Martzolf. Her daughter was a girlfriend of mine in country school.

I feel so sad about little Stanley. There aren't any pictures of me holding him. I missed him for a long time.

Mr. Baglow, Life Insurance Agent

After Stanley Julius died, an insurance agent came to our home. We lived right beside State Highway 11, so it was very convenient for salespersons. Our family was still grieving. By the time the agent left, he had sold my parents life insurance policies for our entire family (both of my parents, Leroy, Florence, Inez, and Gladys). The payment was $24 every four months. These policies kept our family poor as long as they existed! The insurance agent was preying on the misery of a heartbroken, poor family.

I was only eleven years old, but I can still remember the day when the statement for the policies came in our mailbox. We had to sacrifice so many needed things out of our family budget. The only insurance my parents should have had was term insurance.

9

COOKING

German Russia Cooking

When I was growing up, I had to help pick rocks from the field, husk corn, and shock grain. Most of the time, I took care of the yard, and fed the chickens and hogs. I was in charge of our household by the age of ten. By the time I was thirteen, I was doing a great deal of the cooking.

In the spring, the potato supply was low, some of our seasonal food was running out, and many of our canned vegetables were short. At this time, we turned to our German Russia dough diet. Though we all enjoyed it, these dishes were labor intensive.

I cooked strudels. Sometimes, I made plain strudel and divided it in half. One half remained plain, and the other half had sauerkraut. To complete the meal, I added potatoes and any meat that was available.

We enjoyed the pleasant flavor of Kartoffel Kurbuis Strumbus was made of boiled potatoes, boiled pumpkin, and flour browned in lard. When we combined the ingredients and mashed them, it had a texture like mashed potatoes.

We prepared bread dough early in the morning several days a week. Since schub noodla (dumplings) were made of bread dough, we prepared them the same morning. They were cooked and served at our noon meal. We formed small pieces about the size of an egg, and let them rise for an hour. With an inch of water in the roaster pan, we added diced potatoes, lard, salt and pepper. When this was brought to a boil, the schub noodla were added. We did not lift the cover of the roaster – no peeking for fifteen or twenty minutes. If the cover was lifted, the dumplings would flop into a doughy stage. If necessary, we could reduce the temperature by moving the roaster away from the hotter area of the cookstove.

There were always leftover dumplings. In the afternoon, I prepared a dish by cutting them into small pieces. These were heated and lightly browned in a large, cast iron pan. When I added six eggs and brought it to a hot stage, it became our evening meal.

Other favorites included borscht (vegetable soup), knoephla soup, knoephla and sauerkraut, case knoephla (cheese buttons), and kuchen.

There were no written measurements for our meat and vegetable cooking. I watched my mother cook, and I knew which bowls and kettles she used for the dough dishes. The only recipes I used were for cakes, desserts, and cookies.

In my cooking experience, there was never a complaint from my siblings about food. I think they were fortunate they had anything to eat.

German Russia Dough Dishes, Food Preservation

My family grew up on German food from Russia. My ancestors invented all the dough dishes that we enjoyed. All those dishes were a product of the flour barrel and the salted pork barrel. If you threw a few eggs in there, it was complete. If they didn't have anything else, they did have that.

There was no way of preserving food. If they were lucky, they had an outdoor food cellar about eight to ten feet deep where they could store potatoes, beets, carrots, and some meats. If they had water seepage at that level, however, this was not possible.

Closing-Quick Meal Stove – A Life Saved

My mother always wanted a new kerosene stove to replace her old, three-burner stove. She bought a forty-inch-wide, streamlined, white porcelain stove. It had four wick burners in the cooktop, and two wick burners underneath the oven door. It was a beautiful stove indeed.

She traded Ashley Shock Hardware Store a milk cow. Her name was Bessie. I don't know if it was an even trade. However, Mr. Shock delivered the stove to our home in a trailer, and then loaded Bessie in the trailer and took her away.

The company that manufactured the stove named it "Quick Meal." We enjoyed the stove. It made our home look modern. One day, the family was out doing the chores and milking the cows. When we came into the house, the burners had burned up and created a black smoke. There was zero visibility — the walls, curtains, furniture, and everything in the room was affected. This happened more than once. Sometimes, the doors to all the bedrooms were open, and the whole house was soot.

I was about fourteen at the time, and scrubbed the walls many times. Eventually, we closed the doors, so the smoke did not get into the bedrooms and living room. My mother spoke to Mr. Shock, but he did not have any answer for our problem. Later, she found out the reason the stove burners burned and created smoke was due to a lack of oxygen.

We also noticed there was a leak in one of the oven burners. It was a slow drip of kerosene. My mother placed a small, porcelain dish under the drip. Stanley Roger, my little brother, was about eighteen months or two years old. He would get into the lower drawer and play with the kettles. I think he already knew then that he was going to be a diesel engineer. I saw him as a brat always into something.

One morning, my mother was doing some work in the basement, and I was in the kitchen washing dishes. I saw Stanley open the door to the oven burners. He grabbed the little dish that had a few drops of kerosene in it, and put it to his mouth. While he was trying to spit it out, he passed out!

I screamed, "Mother! Stanley is dead!"

She came up from the basement, lifted him up, and held him in her arms. She said, "Father is in town with the car. Run to town!"

I started to run on the gravel road. I ran a mile. I had never run this fast or this far. I met Father and said, "Stanley swallowed kerosene, and I think he is dead." When I got into the car, we raced home.

Father said, "We are going to Ashley to the doctor."

However, the tires on our car were wartime tires, and were in very poor condition. My parents rushed Stanley to our neighbor, Gust Schlepp. He had purchased a new car, and volunteered to take them to the doctor seven miles away.

The doctor rapidly administered an enema. When Stanley displayed instant signs of recovery, my parents were greatly relieved!

One of the first things my parents did was to get rid of the "Quick Meal" stove. It ended up on the junk pile. The next stove Mother purchased was a Maytag bottled gas, cooking stove. It was a beautiful, good stove and she used it as long as they lived on the farm.

Grandfather Dockter, Butchering and Canning a Cow

My father, Julius, described how his father, Gottlieb Jr., used to sit at the kitchen table with a kerosene light at his side and read. One day, he had been stocking supplies and had purchased a box of canning jars. There were processing charts and instructions on how to can vegetables, fruit, and meat.

He was curious about preserving meat. He followed the instructions and was amazed at how tasty canned beef was. At that time, there was no refrigeration and no way to preserve beef in the summertime. Canned beef was the answer!

His next project was butchering and canning a beef cow. The canning process he used was hot water bath, and the containers were Atlas quart and half gallon canning jars. He was excited there was a way to provide a supply of good meat for his family in the hottest time of the year.

Dear Grandma, Cookstove and Mischt

Dear Grandma Katie,

I am going back to 1936 after my sister, Inez, was born. My parents bought a building from the Andrew Haas family. It was a small house in which Uncle Andrew and his wife, Magdalena, had previously lived. (Magdalena was my father's sister.)

Uncle Andrew and his wife built a new house, and then moved out of the small house. Before it was moved to the Julius Dockter farm, it was used as a chicken coop. It now served as a new kitchen and hall entry for us, and added a lot of space to our house!

Our cookstove was a very expensive appliance, and took up a lot of room. It served as a heater for our home, and also had a large area for kettles to cook. The top six lids were made of heavy, cast iron. The top of the stove had a reservoir which attached to the side of the stove. It was very handy to have warm water all the time! The fire crates were under the front two lids. There was a handle for opening this area which allowed us to feed the materials for burning. We could burn almost anything: wood, coal, paper, cow plasters that we picked up in the pasture, and the all-famous, cured and dried manure called "mischt." We used a shaker handle to shake ashes out of the fire crates. This stove required a lot of maintenance.

In cold weather, the fastest way to bank and start the cookstove was to go out to the pigpen and gather the dry corncobs which pigs had left. After using corncobs, paper, or lightweight wood to start the cookstove fire, we could add mischt. Coal was good for lasting heat.

We did not use our cookstove in the summer except to heat the sad irons which we used for ironing clothes. I used a small iron for handkerchiefs, while my mother used the heavy irons. My iron was about three inches long and one and a half inches wide. I thought it was a toy — but it was not. It's real purpose was to flatten small pleats in ruffles.

In the summer months, we used our kerosene stove. It had three burners and a convertible oven which could be placed on top of two burners. It was used to bake bread and cake in the summertime because it did not give off a lot of heat. The name of the company that made this stove was "Florence."

In the winter, our horses and cows were sometimes fed behind the barn. This created a ply of hay and fresh animal droppings. We unloaded horse and cow manure on this ply. We also added pig manure, chicken house straw, and manure LeRoy removed from the barn shed.

I vaguely remember my father preparing this manure bed for drying. He waited until after the summer rains in July or August to begin the pack of the ply. A packer was made from a threshing machine cylinder. When it was all put together, it became a roller. Father hitched Queen and Butte to this packer, and the hooves of the horses helped to mix the manure. It became a whole pile of mixed "shit" about twelve to fourteen inches deep. This process was necessary, and continued until the end of August.

The ply became firm. Our mother and father started to spade squares about 12" x 12," and set them diagonally so they could continue to dry out and cure. After a week, the squares could be put into shocks, and more drying and curing took place. The last step was to store them in a dry shed for winter use. The mischt was now ready for the cookstove.

When I was about two years old, my parents were preparing the manure ply. They were using two horses hitched to a wagon, standing in the middle of the ply. I was sitting and playing under this wagon. When the horses moved a little, the wagon wheel went over my body at the waist. The way my father told the story, I was not permanently hurt. However, I had back problems later in life. Then Father always said, "It is still is from the time when she got run over by the wagon wheel on the mischt!"

The mischt was a handy, cheap, much-needed byproduct that was used in the cookstove for heating and cooking. The only other source of heat we had in our house was a parlor, coal heater in the living room.

My Mother-In-Law

I don't know much about Sophie, my mother-in-law. I know she was a strong, courageous person. Reason has it that she proved it by the life she lived. I had the privilege of working with her when she came with Grandfather Matt to help restore the rundown farm that Art and I leased from them. I always had the feeling that Sophie liked me and my babies.

She often talked about her life when she and I were alone. When she was sixteen, she and her younger brother came to America from the Ukraine in the South Russia area. One of her jobs in the United States was to plow a field with horses. Crops were so poor there was no hay or grain to feed the horses. The farmers went to the grain centers and bought grain chaff which was composed of weeds, grain, and other discards. They baked these ingredients into loaves of bread. The horses knew they were going to be fed a loaf of bread at each end of the field. This was the only feed that was available for them at that time. Times were hard. The horses were hungry.

Sophie and Matt Rudolph got married and claimed homestead in 1906. On September 7, 1918, she gave birth to her sixth child, Arthur. Matt had an older brother, John, who lived seven miles south of them. In January 1919, John Rudolph's wife gave birth to her thirteenth child, Julius. However, she died in childbirth. When Matt and Sophie received the death notice of John's wife, the decision was made that Sophie would breast-feed Arthur and Julius until the babies could be put on the only formula available, cow's milk. Eventually, the family took horses and wagon and safely returned baby Julius to the John Rudolph farm.

Life was not easy for anyone in a large family. The oldest son in the John Rudolph's family was John Jr. He was thirteen when his mother died. Imagination can tell what the life of the farm boy was like in his position as the oldest son. There was also a sister who was twelve and she had eleven younger siblings.

In those days, there was no money and no hospital. Sometimes, there was no doctor within twenty miles. The nearest trading center was also twenty miles away. Sophie felt that someone had to help look after the John Rudolph's family. So, she hitched horses to a wagon, took her baby, and drove seven miles to the John Rudolph farm. She made several trips to see how the new baby, Julius, was coming along.

In time, John married a widow with five children. Later, he and his wife, Carrie, had three more children. That was a total of twenty-one.

Later, my husband and I owned the Matt Rudolph family farm. There was an evangelical church one mile east of our farm. That is where the families of Matt and John Rudolph attended church. Every year, the families who still lived in the community would gather for spring church and cemetery cleanup before Memorial Day. One year, a community event conflicted with the annual workday. Only one of the members, Bill Schuler, and I showed up at the church. We decided to clean the cemetery as well as time allowed, and let others finish the job. Mr. Schuler was a very knowledgeable person. He knew the people and community well.

The fence around the cemetery was made of wood posts and barbed wire which was usually broken down by snow in the winter. While we were doing repairs, I noticed there was a grave marker on the outside of the fence. I pointed the marker out to Mr. Schuler. The marker said, "John Rudolph Jr., Age 20."

I said, "Why is that marker outside of the cemetery fence?"

He hesitated. Then he said, "Well, see, he committed suicide, and our church feels that taking your life interferes with the will of God."

I was spellbound because I knew the story of how John's mother had died when he was thirteen. I thought it was unfair that the church did not recognize the fact that John Jr. had a hard life, and may have had a nervous breakdown. He was engaged to a young lady, and, shortly before he died, she broke off the engagement. His father, John Sr., was not a kind man.

Several years after that Memorial Day, the church put a new steel fence around the rural Methodist Cemetery. The John Rudolph Jr. grave marker was on the inside of the cemetery fence.

Times were relentless for the families that filed homestead claims. If the settlers arrived in late fall, the North Dakota ground was already starting to freeze. To survive, they had to dig a hole in the ground, and that was where they lived until spring. Farms had to be built to endure the cold winters. There were no roads, no trees, no shelter of any kind.

The only transportation they had was horses or oxen, a wagon and a sleigh. There were no cars.

There was no place to store food — no way to keep food supplies. Eventually, they had hogs to butcher. The housewife or cook would become creative. My mother-in-law, Sophie, told me one time that often there was no meat of any kind for her family of eleven children. She would go out to the pigpen, catch and butcher a twenty-pound feeder pig, and cook pork for the evening meal! I'm sure her children helped her catch the porker.

Between the pork barrel and the flour barrel, there were many tasty, hunger-satisfying dishes created! Just the thought of her solving the problem of putting food on the table made her a "noble pioneer woman."

A Pioneer Woman

The North Dakota State Hospital was built in 1885. It was an institution to treat mentally ill patients. There were 2,000 patients who were pioneer women. Why so many women?

Most of the settlers who came to the Dakota area arrived from Europe and the neighboring area of Ukraine. They lived in colonies. These were divided into dorfs that formed small villages. The men worked in the surrounding area tilling the fields, harvesting the crops, and tending the cattle and the forest. The women lived in the center of the dorfs in their homes. They were close to their children. They took care of the gardens and animals. They always had a neighborhood surrounding their community, and were close to relatives and friends.

When the immigrants came in the 1880s, most of them had saved all their money to pay for the fare to come to America on a ship. They needed a sponsor to open a home for them. They were advised to stake a homestead claim for 160 acres of land. In order to claim ownership, they needed to build a 10' x 12' claim shack, and live there five years.

They did not know where this claim was located in the township. The location of towns had not been established. The railroad may not have been close. Some of them lived forty miles from a trading post. There were no roads and no hospitals. There were miles and miles of prairie, and nothing but prairie. After a while, they had to accept the fact that they were in isolation.

They needed transportation. They had to have horses, oxen, or mules to get to a trading post. Many times, it took more than four days for a round-trip. While all these business trips were going on, the women were left at home tending to the few meager properties they had in their possession. They were in complete isolation, and perhaps had small children. She taught them to gather eggs from the prairie chickens that roamed the prairie, and to take only one egg a day in order not to destroy the hen's hatch. This was the beginning of the life of the pioneer woman.

As they began to farm, many times she led the oxen for her husband when they broke the sod. Sometimes, she followed the plowshare and turned the sod. After a long day in the field, she went home to milk the cow. After that, she worried what she was going to prepare for her family's evening meal.

Once the family became established, some things did not change much for women. Most kitchens had a cookstove with a big, black top. Some stoves had white, light green, or blue porcelain fronts and trim. Some had chrome trim. Some were all black. No matter what the color was, they all had a big black top. She had to bring in wood and burn material to build a fire. That was where she cooked and baked. She planted, watered, and weeded her garden; then harvested potatoes and many other vegetables. She made cabbage into sauerkraut, baked bread, and cured meat. She churned butter if she had a churner. If she did not, she put cream in a gallon can with a tight lid, and shook the container until butter was formed.

She sewed clothes for her large family. Since there was no sewing machine, she stitched them by hand. She also knit clothing for them. She had to get water from the well, and heat it to wash the clothes on a washboard. She ironed with the heavy, sad irons.

The mortality rate of children was high in the days of the pioneer woman. This was also a stress factor in her life. Though she gave birth to the sons who defended this country in war, she did not have the right to vote.

In those days, men could go to town to do business or could go to a bar and socialize. Women were not allowed in a bar. They had limited areas to socialize. Some women were at the mercy of the behavior of their husbands. Domestic violence was hidden and not reported. Some cultures taught their daughters to deny their spouse had bad behavior, and to cover up their problems. They felt they could do nothing about it.

Sometimes, the work, hardship, and loneliness the pioneer woman endured on the prairie was more than a life could bear. The result was a nervous breakdown, and she was admitted to the state hospital for treatment. Sadly, medicine for treatment was not available. Many patients never recovered well enough to be released.

Dear Grandma, Forever Yeast–"Avigar Sautz"

Dear Grandma Katie,

When settlers came from the mother country, they brought their recipe of Forever Yeast with them. It consisted of potato water and sugar which fermented at room temperature. When they added flour and baked it, they had wonderful bread. Every household had flour. If they did not have flour, they could not exist.

I remember my mother preparing to bake bread when I was a child. Because the grocery store did not stock it, this was a chore that had to be done at least once a week. She brought out her big, bread dough pan. The recipe was in her head. She knew how many cups of flour she needed — how much sugar and salt.

There was always a quart jar of Forever Yeast which the German Russians called Avigar Sautz. She stirred the yeast in the jar, and carefully poured half of it into the flour mixture. She saved the other half, and refilled the jar with more potato water and sugar. This kept the yeast fermenting so it could be used the next week to bake bread. She then proceeded to mix and knead the dough.

Many times, we had fried bread for lunch. These were chunks of yeast dough, deep-fried in pork lard. Today, Indians use this tasty, fried bread for making Indian tacos.

10

THE CHICK PROJECT

My first memories of chickens on our farm involve a special shed. It was a small building to house hens when they became broody in the spring. It had four compartments, and each had a little door. I may have been five or six at the time, but I could not get into them. They were too small.

My mother built a nest in each compartment. She put twenty-one chicken eggs in each box of hay, and waited until dark. A broody hen was placed on the nest, and a basket was put over her. After twenty-four hours, she became acclimated to her nest in the daylight. There were four hens set to hatch a total of eighty-four eggs.

My job was to supply water for each hen. If they did not get water on a hot day, they would abandon their eggs, and just sit beside the nest. The eggs would become cold and never hatch.

It was a joy to watch the eggs hatch. The hen (we called her a cluck) watched each little chick as it emerged under her. She claimed every one! After all of them had hatched, she wanted to get out of the cluck house. She walked her little baby chicks into the grass to show them food in the soil and grass. She would pick and chirp, and all the babies ran to see what the mother cluck had found. It did not take her long to teach the babies to feed themselves.

It took about two weeks for the young chicks to lose their soft, fuzzy feathers. They grew new feathers, and went into the ugly duckling stage. My mother kept a close eye on the chicks as they grew, and they were also under the eye of the cluck. Mother thought some of the chicks were not developing as they should. She caught some, examined them, and confirmed her suspicion. The chicks had lice. There were no chemicals for such pests at that time. She caught them one at a time, greased them with goose lard, found the nits, and crushed them with her thumb and fingernails. As the chicks ran and played in the dust and wind, they turned gray and dirty. They had lost all their charm and glamour.

They outgrew that stage, and developed into full feather stage. By then, the cluck lost track of her baby chicks. She could not recognize them anymore. By the 4th of July, boy chicks were roosters and tried to crow. They were ready to be butchered for fried chicken. The girl chicks lived on to lay eggs, and continued to be laying hens for about two years.

As the chicken industry process modernized, hen hatching became outdated. It became much easier to order our baby chicks from the hatchery.

It was then that Father planned to make a building large enough for 300 baby chicks. He took down the cluck house, and bought a building that had been used as a coal shed for a country school. It was not large enough, so he built on a lean-to. This doubled the size, and made a large, brooder house with a low-pitched roof.

As we enlarged our chicken industry, we encountered some surprises. Our chicks were ordered to arrive the first week of May. After the brooder house was ready, there had to be a brooder heater for the nights and cold spells in North Dakota. The kerosene heater had a circle shield about eight feet in diameter, and stood about eight inches off the floor. The baby chicks all huddled around the brooder heater. There was only a dim light at night, and they all slept. Mother and I always made one more trip to the chicken house before we turned in at night.

One stormy night, a strong wind blew out the flame on the kerosene burner. The wind blast was too much for the little chimney. The brooder house was soon cold without the heater, and all the little chicks began to huddle together. They soon became a pile. By the time we found out what had happened, half of them had suffocated. There were layers of dead chicks. It was a sad disaster. Mother placed an order to replace them, and we started over again.

There was also a problem with cannibalism: if the chicks were over-crowded, or if there was any injury on a chick (sometimes caused by the pecking order). If there was a drop of blood for them to taste the flesh, it was easy for one chick to pick the skin of another chick. This was a constant threat the first few days when they were in the brooder house.

The chicks grew up in the brooder house until they were almost mature. At this stage, male and female could be identified. As was mentioned previously, the males were fryers and the females were egg layers.

After eight weeks, the males were large enough to be butchered. Soon, we had fried chicken. It was a nice change, and a break from beef, pork sausage, and head cheese.

It took about 45 minutes to prepare a chicken for dinner, our noon meal of the day. Sometimes, it took longer to catch the chicken than to prepare it. I would take what we called a chicken hook. This was a wire approximately five feet long with a small, curved piece of metal at the end. It would hook a chicken by one foot, so it could be caught. Once the chicken was in my hand, I stepped on both wings with one foot, and on both legs with the other foot. I held the head with one hand and a knife in the other hand, and would cut the head off. After I let it go, the chicken would jump until it was done bleeding.

The next step was to plunge it into boiling water for one minute, so the feathers could be removed. It was then ready for the inner organs to be removed, and the chicken was cut up into pieces. The cooking time was one hour.

Back to the brooder house. The chickens were almost fully grown by then, and the room was getting too small despite all the male chicks that were prepared for meals. It was time to move them over to the hen house which was to become their permanent home.

This was a family project. We closed the brooder house one day until it was dark. By then, the grown chicks were looking for a place to sleep. As a family, we joined hands, and tried to herd the them over to the hen house. This was usually a comedy – like herding cats. The second night was much easier because they remembered their roosts from the previous night. They didn't know it, but they were naturally made to roost.

It took twenty-one days for chicken eggs to hatch, twenty-seven days for duck eggs, and thirty days for goose eggs. The broody hens were also set to hatch duck eggs and goose eggs. Had they known that they were being used, they would have been madder than "wet hens."

This final building stood in the Julius Dockter farmyard for many years — after all the other buildings were either moved away or fell to pieces. Our farm was located nine miles west of Ashley, North Dakota, on State Highway 11.

The chick project was a major factor our family's financial support. The fresh eggs we sold every week paid for our groceries and other family needs.

PS. I almost forgot the many, many times I cleaned the droppings and wet straw that had to be removed as the chickens grew and needed more room. My father, my mother, siblings (LeRoy, Inez, Gladys, Stanley), and I all had a part in the chick project.

Father Getting Chickens To Lay Eggs

Father did not usually spend much time inside the house. However, there were many days when we were blocked in by blizzards. There was no place to go on a blizzard day, and they were long days for him. After the chores were done, he was usually just in the house waiting for the evening chores to come.

One day, he came out of his bedroom, and picked up the tea kettle which was always on the cooking stove. He took the boiling water, and went out to the chickens to thaw out their water troughs. When he came to the water troughs, he noticed the chickens came running. After that, he timed it so that they always had warm water.

When their water was frozen, the chickens could not drink. But when warm water was provided, they drank a lot. As a result, the chickens started to lay eggs just as they did in the summer months! The settlers thought it took warm weather for chickens to lay eggs, but this was not true.

In the past, my mother used to reserve a large case of eggs for our winter use. After my father's discovery, we had eggs not only to use, but also to sell in the winter months!

The Treacherous Turn – State Highway 11 / County Road

Our farm was beside Highway 11 that met a quiet, county road leading into Venturia. Too many accidents took place at this corner. Drivers could not see well in blizzards. If they missed their turn, they got stuck in the snow or drove into a ditch. If they were stuck or their vehicles would no longer run, they would cautiously walk to our nearby farm seeking help.

Often, this would happen at night. They pounded on our door. Father would get out of bed, get dressed for cold weather, go to the barn and harness the horses. He "drove" to the corner and either pulled out their car or pulled it so it would start. If there was a blizzard and everything failed, Father would bring the stranded people into our home. Mother would get up and help bed them down. Many times, she also provided breakfast for them.

We lived in a two-bedroom home. Once, the blizzard lasted three days and six people stayed at our home. Another night, a blizzard came up without warning and fourteen people were unexpectedly stuck in the snow. All these people stayed in our home! We did not fear to take them in. We needed each other. At this time, people were kind and helped each other. Though they were total strangers, our parents took them in.

One summer day, a man came running to our farm and summoned our father to the corner. There had been a serious accident. A man was in a car and had many glass cuts over his body. One cut was at the jugular vein in his throat. I don't know what kind of car Father had when he rushed that man to the doctor nine miles away. My guess is that it was our Model A Ford. Father saved the man's life.

After this accident, the county sheriff came to our farm and thanked Father for saving the man. In casual conversation, the sheriff mentioned the bleeding from the jugular vein. He indicated there should have been some first aid done to prevent heavy bleeding.

Father had his hands in his hip pockets and commented, "Well, you know, if it's an arm or a leg, you can use a tourniquet. But if it's the neck, there is not much you can do."

Father was always a giving person. He gave away more than he had. He purchased a hammer mill to grind dry corn stocks and hay that were too course and not suitable to feed the livestock. It was powered by the flywheel of a tractor. Though it was a handy and expensive piece of machinery in its day, Father's farm was not profitable enough to use it. He loaned the mill without charge to his brothers and neighbors. Eventually, this hammer mill was hammered to pieces and could no longer be repaired.

Father enjoyed making things out of nothing. He constructed a two-wheeled, trailer using an axle with rubber tires. He also let everyone use this trailer until the tires wore out.

Our Flock of Sheep

I was nine years old in 1940. That was the time when the rains came back. Farmers were beginning to get back into the mixed farming they had to get out of during the dust storms of the 1930s. They increased the milk cow herd, hogs, poultry, sheep, and other animals that consumed feed like oats and barley. My father had a flock of thirty sheep. There were about thirty ewes and one ram.

Lambing season was a busy time in the spring. Father was in the barn many nights to watch the lambs being born. Sheep are poor mothers. Many times, they do not claim their newborns. Sometimes, they have twins or triplets, but will only claim one lamb. There was a small pen in the barn that looked like a box. Father would put the ewe and her lambs in the box until she could recognize her babies. When lambs were six or seven months old, they were sold at a livestock sale as a cash crop.

The mother sheep produced wool. Father hired a professional sheep shearer who was trained to shear without cutting or damaging the skin. He could hold and shear the sheep in a matter of minutes. Then, he would roll each sheep's wool, fold it, and tie it in a bundle.

One year, the inspector did not buy Father's sheep wool because it was infested with cockleburs. This is a noxious weed that grew everywhere, especially in rich soil like the manure pile. This pile was warm during the cold nights, and that's where the sheep would lay to sleep. Our wool was normally worth about thirty dollars which was a lot of money at that time. It was the month of June, and Father brought the wool home.

Father and LeRoy were making hay at that time. Mother and I took the wool into the barn shed and carefully unrolled each bundle. We searched and pulled the stickery cockleburs out. Sometimes, we had to trim them out with a scissors. We had sore fingers. I don't know how many days she and I worked on that wool. Finally, Mother and I took the wool to town and the inspector bought the wool. It was free of cockleburs.

This weed would have continued to cause the same problem every year. It was the end of our sheep project. Father sold his flock of lambs and sheep that fall. "The cockleburs won."

11

WORLD WAR II

Dear Grandma, World War II

D ear Grandma Katie,
This is what I remember of World War II.
December 7, 1941. It was a Sunday evening. A radio program was interrupted with breaking news that Japanese planes had bombed Pearl Harbor. It was a devastating attack destroying most of our United States naval fleet! Our family and community had no idea how the war would affect us. I was ten years old at the time.

Every family received a letter from the federal government. It stated that all males between the ages of twenty-one and thirty-seven were to register for military service. This was a shock. Father said, "What would they want with me and my five kids?" At that time, our father was thirty-five. Fortunately, he received a farm deferment, and none of the children in our family were old enough for military service.

It did not take long to see the widespread impact the military draft would have in our community. It created a shortage of labor in business: teachers, farm laborers, doctors, nurses, etc. The war with Germany also caused a shortage of farm equipment and cars. When John Deere and McCormick factories stopped producing farm vehicles and machinery and switched to manufacturing tanks and guns for the war, the U.S. farm economy was adversely affected. Ford Motors, Chevy, and other car manufacturers stopped making all cars in order to make war material.

This were already major changes happening in agriculture. After going through the Depression and Dustbowl years, there had been a severe transition time. There were seven years of drought, hail, and grasshoppers. Since hay and grain did not grow in the drought, farmers gave up producing cash crops. The need for draft horses was greatly reduced, and farmers did not increase or replace them – they were not bred to produce colts. It was cheaper to feed a cow than a horse, so they increased their milk cows for more cash sale of butterfat.

One Saturday night, when we were on our way home from town, my father was telling Mother what he had just heard. We always had to be quiet when Father was talking. There was a threat — if we were noisy, we would have to stay home after that. So, we overheard everything that he said. We did not compromise anything. We were silent. Father heard in town that several farmers had lost all their horses to a disease called Encephalitis. This caused a severe shortage of horses.

Wheat was ready for harvest. Some farmers were planning to harvest with machinery that was powered with tractors. This was much more economical than feeding horses. Tractors were cheap to operate. Gasoline was $0.10 a gallon. The problem was . . . there were few tractors to be bought!

Father knew that his horses were growing old. He got them in his dowry in 1926. He didn't know how old they were when he got them. Some of them were close to twenty years old in 1941.

One day, Father came home from Ashley, and had purchased a John Deere tractor. The tractor was delivered the next day and looked like a turtle. It had wide, set-out wheels with huge airplane tires on the back. The front wheels were close together (row crop wheels). It was almost impossible to drive, and did not last long on our farm. It cost $800, which was a fortune at the time.

We harvested a good crop in 1942. Our crops were bindered with a horse-drawn machine which cut and tied the grain stock into a bundle. Then, we had to set them into shock piles. When I was six years old, I had to hold the first bundle, and Mother and my brother would set up the bundles around me. I was afraid they would cover me up with the bundles.

Our father and his brothers, Albert and Edwin, owned a thresh machine. A thresher was a big machine driven by the flywheel of a large tractor or steam engine. The machine operated like a large grain combine, but was stationary and had to be pulled from one field to another. It took two men to manage the thresher and engine. Four or five men loaded and brought the wheat bundles to the thresher to pitch them into the mouth or feeder. One man hauled and stored the grain when it came out of the thresher. The days and hours were long, and it was slow, hard, tedious work. Many times, workers who were not used to hard work suffered from physical exhaustion and low salt. They had to discontinue their job.

My mother and I would prepare meals when the threshing crew came to our farm. Breakfast was served at 4:30 in the morning. The menu was prepared, and we served cereal, eggs, cheese (if available), canned olives (if available), sausage, and head cheese. We never served potatoes for breakfast. My mother said potatoes for "noon lunch" and dinner was enough.

At 10 o'clock, Mother and I sent lunch and coffee, pop, or Kool-Aid, rolls, and kuchen to the fields to hold them until the noon meal.

The menu for the noon meal included soup, one meat (beef, pork, or chicken), potatoes (scalloped, mashed, fried, or boiled), cabbage and apples with whipped cream, baked rice and raisins, boiled rice with crushed pineapple and whipped cream, and pigs in the blanket (huloopsa). This meal always included a lot of vegetables from the garden, and canned vegetables and fruit.

At 4 o'clock in the afternoon, we sent lunch to the workers: sandwiches, pickles, pastries, cake, and cookies — anything that was available to hold them for the evening dinner at 10 p.m. The evening meal was like the noon meal. And we always had dessert to complete the meal.

The day also was also long for Mother and me. In addition to cooking and serving meals for the workers, we were milking cows, taking care of the chores, and trying to find time to butcher chickens when we planned to serve chicken the next day.

After the crop was harvested in 1942, there was a crisis. We had just harvested the best crop in the last ten years, but there was no one to thresh the grain because the men were in military service.

I do not know how Father heard people talking about workers coming from Minnesota looking for work in North Dakota. These men got draft deferments. Some were teachers or they were older than draft age, etc. However, they were eager to work and earn money. I doubt that any of them knew how hard they were going to work in the threshing crew.

Father and his brothers, Albert and Edwin, hired four of these men. They called them hobos men. About this time, there were shortages of almost everything. Shelves in the grocery store were almost empty. The threshing started at Albert's farm. Then they moved to Edwin's farm. After finishing there, they moved past our farm! They moved onto Uncle Emil's farm. I remember how frustrated Mother was because they did not stop at our farm to thresh our fields. Father allowed them to pass our farm. He was always a "yes-man." The consequences were tragic this time.

The threshing had gone well with the men from Minnesota and the team finished Uncle Emil's farm on a Saturday night. In those days, no one worked in the field on Sunday. It was not allowed in our Christian principles. It began to rain on Sunday night, and rained for three days. Days were cloudy, and it rained more and more. This went on for two weeks. The hobos lived at our farm, and slept in the hay mow of the barn. Mother and I cooked for them every day. However, they were bored living with us on the farm. There was nothing for them to do. Our house was small, they did not have a car, and the sun did not shine.

One of the men who got a deferment was a teacher. Minnesota had delayed their schools opening because of the labor shortage. But his deferment had expired, and he needed to go back to teaching. One day, he was sitting in the kitchen watching Mother and I getting dinner ready. I was setting the table.

He said to Mother, "Mrs. Dockter, your daughter is doing the work of a sixteen-year-old girl." I was eleven.

At that time, my sister, Inez, was five years old. Our parents told her to sing "You Are My Sunshine." She was so cute because she had a lisp (she had sucked on a pacifier too long). The "sunshine" song had just come out and everybody was singing it. The teacher asked my parents, "Does Florence sing?"

They said, "No." I taught Inez to sing the song!

By then, it was obvious that threshing would be delayed, and the hobos wanted to get back to Minnesota. Father offered to take them back home for a visit with their families. He took them to Crosby, Minnesota, for a three-day visit. The teacher stayed home with his family, and went back to teaching.

Three of the men planned to come back with Father. One of them was retired. Another was a tall, blonde, young man who never talked. The third was a small, middle-aged man who had some musical talent. He had teamed up with another band, and they had sponsored a dance at Venturia.

After visiting at their homes, Father and the three men that had planned to return were on their way back to North Dakota. One of the men from Minnesota was driving the car. When they went through Wadena, Minnesota, they got broadsided by someone who ran a red light. Two of them were seriously hurt, and returned to their homes. The retired man was the only one who was able to return to North Dakota with Father.

The 1941 Ford was badly damaged. We were happy when insurance said it was repairable because there were not any cars to be bought until after the war. After Father came home, the weather cleared up, and the sun came out. By then, however, the grain shocks that were left in the field had started to spoil! The seeds in the sheaves sprouted, and there was no grain value in the seeds. Father lost all his crop.

In 1944, a hailstorm came through our farm. The hail and water were so high, we had to wear overshoes. We were at our Uncle Emil's farm, and watched the hailstorm move toward our farm. When we came home, Mother told me to get a cream pail (which we used to store cream) from the cellar. I went down the stairs. When I was half down on the steps, I could see one wall of the cellar was caved in and there was four feet of water! Boxes, buckets, and cans were floating everywhere. What a shock. The crop was a total loss again.

In 1945, a heavy rain came through the area. It was so hard that our parents held pillows against the windows for fear the windows would break. It sounded like a sleet rain. Wheat was in the heading stage, but did not appear to be damaged by the sleet storm. Three days after the rain, Father drove past a wheat field, and noticed that the wheat did not look good. After examining the wheat stems, he found that the hail had punctured the stems. The sheaves and kernels did not develop, and the crop was a total loss. Those were lean years. What was so hard to take was the fact that the hail seemed to center in Father's land.

For some time, the government had been issuing ration stamps to avoid hoarding and the black market. Food rationing did not affect us much because we could produce meat and vegetables on our farm. However, Mother's relatives lived in Minneapolis, Minnesota. Her sisters sent their fruit stamps to our family, and Mother sent meat and vegetable stamps to her sisters that lived in the cities. Our first food ration was pineapple. We did not know that pineapple grew in Hawaii.

The price of farm products went up! There was a shortage of grain, and most food products were needed to support the war material that was needed. Wheat more than doubled in price. The price of butterfat went up to $2 a pound (double the price we got before). The price of a bushel of flax seed for linseed oil was $14 a bushel. This price was higher than ever in history due to the shortage of oil. We were asked to save all fat drippings to help with manufacturing war material.

There were few clothes to be bought. I went to Confirmation School in 1944. It was traditional for girls to wear all white clothes and white shoes on the final Sunday of the confirmation in church. My mother and I started to search for a white dress weeks before the Confirmation Day. We could not find a white dress or a yard of white fabric — not even a white bedsheet. There were no pastel, colored dresses available. Most of the girls in the class had pastel dresses or handed-down white dresses. We purchased light blue fabric for my dress. It was a sad day for me. As I mentioned before, there was a language barrier that affected the class that year.

There were shortages of everything: building materials, machinery parts, shoes, tires, and furniture. One lady used the fabric of a white parachute to make her wedding dress! The nylon fabric was perfect. To my knowledge, she still has the dress. The Sears Roebuck mail order catalogs featured panties with a waist side button. There was no rubber available for elastic.

World War II changed the world. It created jobs for women like Rosie the riveter. My sister-in-law, Emma, got a job as a riveter. She was a strong, farm girl, and the pay was good. Lady teachers could get married and not lose their jobs (as was customary). After women were allowed to enter the workforce, America grew stronger as an industrial country. The men and women that served in the military paid the price for the horrible conflict of World War II.

Helen Esch (10) Carey Esch (9) Edyth (8) Henry (5) Edna (7)
(Backeter)   (Heiden)   (nelson)

Father: Henry died in 1917 Elm

mother: Katie Heikenstein – Esch – Ritter

My mother's family

Grandparents of Julius Dockler (Joie's Grandpa)
• Parents of Christina Vilhauer: Julius's mother
Grandma
Christina Nee Grozhaus
- 2nd marriage : Wall
- 3rd marriage : Wahle

The Farm I grew up on

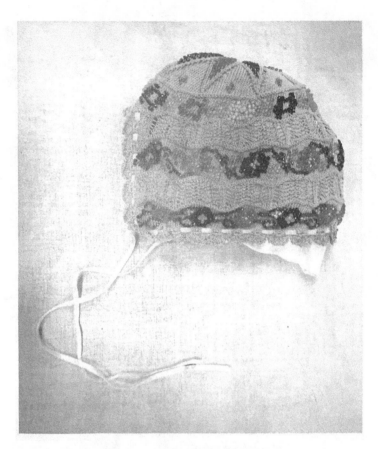

Christine Vilhauer knit the cap

Chicken Barn

Document
No. 4435   Gottlieb Dochter Jr.

Exhibit - 17

UNITED STATES
—TO—

(4-405)

HOMESTEAD PATENT.

THE UNITED STATES OF AMERICA

Homestead Certificate
No. 4752

Application
7438

To all to whom these Presents shall Come, Greeting:

WHEREAS, There has been deposited in the General Land Office of the United States a Certificate of the Register of the Land Office at Bismarck, North Dakota whereby it appears that, pursuant to the Act of Congress, approved 20th May, 1862, "To Secure Homesteads to Actual Settlers on the Public Domain," and the Acts supplemental thereto, the claim of _Gottlieb Dockter Junior_ has been established and duly consummated, in conformity to law, for the _South half of the North West Quarter and the Lots numbered three and four of Section three in Township one hundred and twentynine north of Range seventy-one West of the 5th Principal Meridian in North Dakota; containing one hundred and fifty-nine acres and forty hundredths of an acre_

according to the Official Plat of the Survey of the said Land, returned to the General Land Office by the Surveyor General.

NOW, KNOW YE, That there is therefore granted by the United States unto the said _Gottlieb Dockter Junior_ the tract of Land above described:

TO HAVE AND TO HOLD THE SAID TRACT OF LAND, With the appurtenances thereof, unto the said _Gottlieb Dockter Junior_ and to his heirs and assigns, forever; subject to any vested and accrued water rights for mining, agricultural, manufacturing or other purposes, and rights to ditches and reservoirs used in connection with such water rights as may be recognized and acknowledged by the local customs, laws and decisions of courts; and also subject to the right of the proprietor of a vein or lode to extract and remove his ore therefrom, should the same be found to penetrate or intersect the premises hereby granted, as provided by law.

IN TESTIMONY WHEREOF, I, _Theodore Roosevelt_ President of the United States of America, have caused these Letters to be made Patent, and the seal of the General Land Office to be hereunto affixed.

GIVEN under my hand, at the City of Washington, the _fifteenth_ day of _May_ in the year of our Lord one thousand eight nine hundred and ninety _three_ and of the Independence of the United States the one hundred and _twenty-seventh_

By the President, T. Roosevelt

By _F. M. McKean_ Secretary.

W. Dakota
Recorded, Vol. 148 Page 249

C H Brush chr
Recorder of General Land Office.

Filed for Record the _8th_ day of _July_ A. D. 1903, at 5 o'clock P. M.
Deeds 216
By _Elbert J. Clyde_ Deputy.
G. D. Gross Register of Deeds.

SEAL
GENERAL LAND OFFICE UNITED STATES

Transfer entered July 13, 1903
Edwin Fulbright
for Auditor

A tribute to my great grandparents Helfenstein for braking the frontier and homestead the hardships they endured when they came to America. They laid the groundwork that we enjoyed in this great country.

KATHARINA (KATIE) HELFENSTEIN
HEINRICH (HENRY) ESCH

ANCESTORS AND
DESCENDANTS
1851-2004

This is my grandparents Helfenstein

My grandmother Katie, Me, and my Daughter Jocie, and My Mom Helen

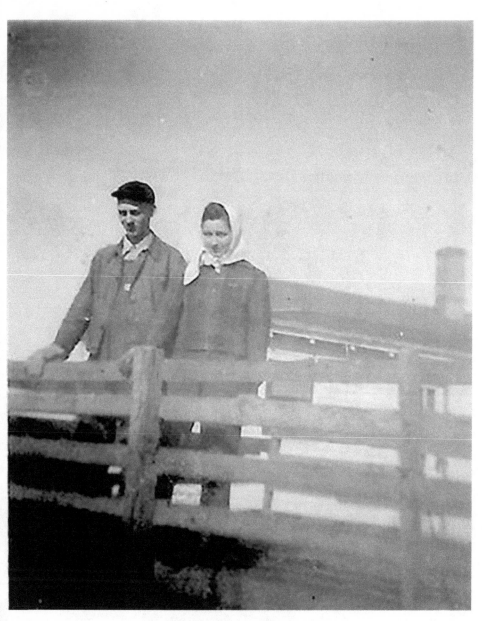

My brother and I hauling hay

School Picnic

My brother and I

My Dear Grandma Katie

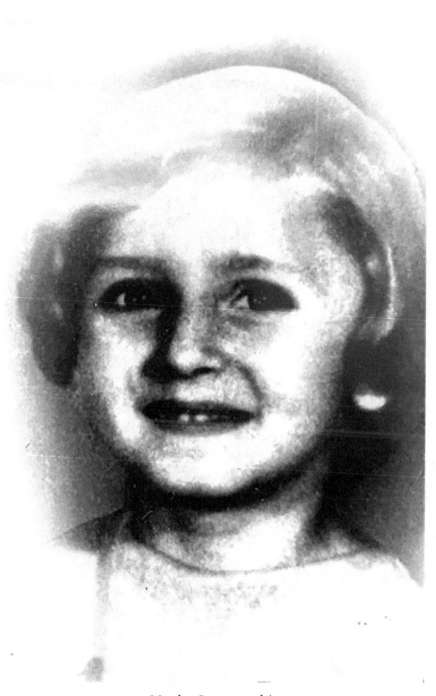

Me when I was around 4

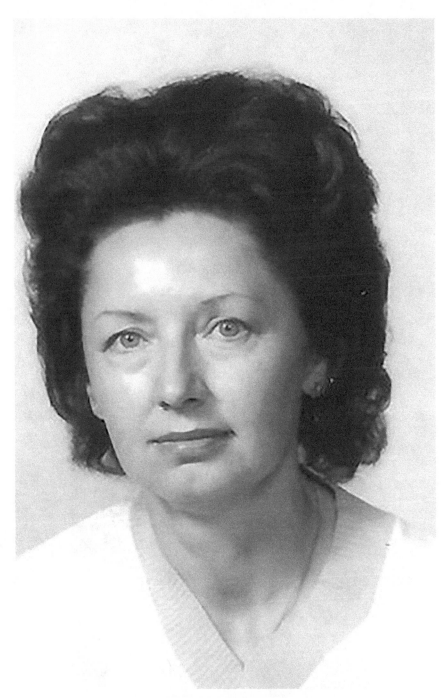

Me when I was in my 40's

Me when I was in my 60's

My father

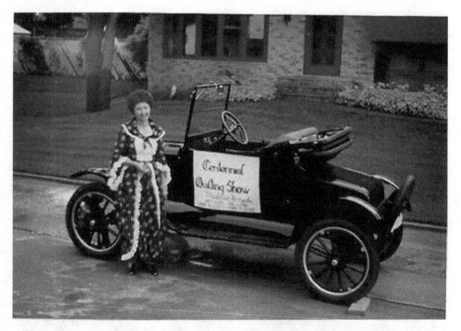

I was Chairmen of Centennial Quilting committee. This is a Martha Washington Dress that I made

1st grade class picture I am in the front center

Paternal Grandfather Gottlieb Docter JR. family portrait

My Parents Helen and Julius Dockter

The farm my husband and I own and operated for 35 years.

12

BEGINNING TRAVEL

Trip to the Twin Cities

It was getting closer to the Christmas holidays. My parents and two younger sisters, Inez and Gladys, had traveled to the Twin Cities in Minnesota for Christmas the year before. It was a memorable train trip including their unforgettable doll purchase of more than one doll for each.

One year later in 1945, I was fourteen. My brother, LeRoy, was sixteen. Our cousin, Virgil Heiden, was the same age as my brother and they were close friends. My mother told me LeRoy and Virgil were thinking about going to the Twin Cities that year for Christmas. The plan was that they would stay at Grandma Katie's home. It was a story and a half house where her boys, George and Clarence, also lived. They were our teenage uncles. The four boys were making plans for their activities.

My mother did not know if I would be going on the train trip with them. She was also wondering where I would be staying and if there was enough money for me to go along. The train fare was $27. LeRoy had obtained his teacher certification after high school and was teaching school. He had purchased a 1935 Ford car and was making payments on it.

After much discussion, the decision was made that I would also go to Minneapolis. LeRoy said he would pay the $27 for my train ticket.

The trip was a thrilling experience. Our farm was located fifty miles south from where the Northern Pacific Railroad was. At that time, there was a special train called the Hiawatha that carried only passengers. We embarked at Dawson, North Dakota. The depot agent told us that he would place a white flag two miles up the track. The train stopped for two seconds and we jumped on! The agent threw our bags on the train and off we went.

There were five passenger cars filled with military servicemen. My Uncle Ben and Aunt Carrie took us to the train depot for departure. Aunt Carrie tactfully warned me about the servicemen. She said, "It is best not to talk to them at all."

My mother's maiden name was Helen Esch, and most of her family lived in Minneapolis, Minnesota, at that time. My Aunt Edna was married to Stanley Crossiant and they had five children. She was 4 feet tall, a petite and pretty lady. Sadly, he was killed in a car accident and left her a young widow. She was my favorite aunt.

Andrew Esch was my mother's brother. He and his wife, Wilma Wolf, and their family lived in Minneapolis. Aunt Elsie and her husband, Art Iversen, and their family also lived in the Twin Cities.

It was exciting to meet these aunts and uncles. Most of them did not know me anymore. I was 5'4" tall and they were short like my mother. I was fourteen and passed for sixteen.

The first night, I stayed at Grandma Katie's beautiful house on Nicolet Avenue. LeRoy, Cousin Virgil, and our two, teen step-uncles, George and Clarence, slept upstairs.

The next night, Aunt Edna invited me to her home. She said, "There will be a party at Uncle Andy's place."

"Is it a birthday party?" I asked.

She said, "No. They are going to have drinks." That sounded good to me.

The next day, we went to a second party. It was at Aunt Elsie's place and the refreshments were the same. We had a wonderful time. My relatives treated and welcomed me like an adult. I liked the attention that I never had in my own home.

One night, I stayed at the Andy Esch home with my cousins, Darlene, Bonnie, and Karma. Grandma Katie and Grandfather Ritter took me to Aunt Elsie and Uncle Art's home for lunch. Elsie was not much of a housekeeper, but she was a wonderful cook. She cooked oxtail soup for lunch. The broth was very tasty. There were large green cabbage leaves, chunky potatoes, carrots, tomatoes, and other vegetables. In conversation at the lunch table, Elsie told us that she had a difficult time locating an oxtail. She had sent her husband all the way to St. Paul to purchase it. While this conversation was going on, we had a good time.

When I got home, I told my mother about the oxtail soup.

She said, "I never heard of such a thing. When we butcher a beef, we throw away the tail."

13

THE WINTER OF 1950

The Winter of 1950

Art and I were married in 1948. The winter of 1948 and 1949 was a new experience for me. We lived twenty miles east of Napoleon, North Dakota. The directions were "sixteen miles east on State Highway #34, and 3½ miles north to the farm." State Highway #34 was maintained by the state of North Dakota. The 3½ miles north to the farm was a section line that separated sections of land where there was no maintenance.

The first winter we lived there, we had average snowfall. We were snowbound most of the time. We did find ways to dig ourselves out, and go to town for supplies and shopping. This was a new, shocking experience for me!

The farm home that I grew up in was beside Highway 11 – a state road that led to a county road that went to Venturia, North Dakota. This was two miles from the North Dakota and South Dakota state line. We went to Venturia Tuesday nights and Saturday nights. I had not been snowed in longer than three days. Sometimes, our parents went up to Venturia with the horses and sleigh to get supplies, and sell eggs and fresh cream. These were the days when cars were not modern. Radiators froze up, and there were no heaters in the car. It was easier to drive over the top of the snow, than to open a road. We always found a way to dig out because we only lived two miles from town.

The first year, the winter had about average snowfall. There were many changes that were unusual for me. I had to adjust to the first year of marriage. I lived fifty miles from the home where I grew up.

The second year, 1950, was a year of "infamy." On December 10, we had ten inches of snow. That was the beginning. There was not one thaw day. More snow and blizzards, and more snow. Farmers could not get feed to their cattle. The field tractors were large, and were in storage. They would not run in the cold temperatures. Small tractors could not maneuver in heavy snow. We ran out of hay and grain for the cattle. We were out of fuel to heat the house. The fuel company, "Farmer's Union", notified the farmers that they would deliver fuel on Highway #34 up to the section lines. Farmers had to come and get the fuel with horses and sleighs, and supply their own barrels.

And it snowed and snowed. One of the neighbors, Fred Schuler, had a large supply of hay. Out of the goodness of his heart, he offered to sell everyone one ton of hay at a reasonable price. There were no telephones then. It was not easy to spread news.

On May 10, we were blessed with the last snow blizzard and ten more inches of snow! There was an estimate of approximately 100 inches of snow in 1950 – 51. According to the news, Canada also had record snowfall in that time period.

We got the news that Fred Schuler had more hay to sell. By then, it was warm enough that the field tractors would start. We had an Oliver 99 Hartpar tractor that may have been twenty years old. We had about forty-five head of cattle, and were completely out of feed. The hardships were showing up in temperament.

After more hay was available, we had to make a decision on how to get it. The old Oliver field tractor was parked beside the chicken coop the last fall. It had a crank handle starter. Art had given up on everything. He walked over to the tractor, pulled the crank up one time, and the tractor started to spit, sputter, and roar. It was running! He hitched the hayrack to the tractor, and went to get more hay!

By then, the roads were mud. After the snow started to melt, we were in for more surprises. That was when the floods began coming from the north, even from Canada! There were floods, then freezes. The low areas, roads, and fields flooded. The floods and freezes created thin ice lakes.

The only machines we had were the family car which was a 1946 Ford that had not been driven for months, a Model A McCormick tractor that would spin on top of the snow and ice, and an old truck that was stored in a shed the last fall.

Back to the hay supply. After the Oliver tractor started, Art left to get more hay at Schuler's. We had six bales left from the first hay supply we bought. We moved those bales close to the house, away from the cattle. While I was walking over to the house, I noticed the cows were walking to the watering tank. We had an old cow whose name was Blossom. (She was one of the six cows I got in my dowry.) She stopped short, put her nose up, and sniffed the air. She flared her nostrils. She could smell the clover in the hay. She made a dash and crashed through the fence. She went straight to the bales, and all the cows followed her! So that was the end of the six bales of hay! We did get some more hay that day.

By then, it was the end of May. We were milking cows, and had to market fresh cream and sell eggs. We had a Model A Ford car that we used as a field car. It was green with no upholstery on the inside. It did have seats in the front and the back. It looked as though it was burned in a fire, but it did run well.

We had to get rid of the farm produce, so we loaded the ten-gallon cream can into the passenger seat of the Model A car, and the egg crates into the backseat. I sat in the backseat. Then we took off for the town of Streeter, North Dakota. Art was driving the car. Napoleon was the town where we normally did most of our business, but at that time, the roads flooded underwater. Many roads were washed out, and not passable. I don't know how we got to Streeter that day. We were driving in fields, section lines, and lakes. We were driving on ice. Sometimes, the car broke through the ice. We did not stop. We were in water, but just kept on driving. Art was driving with one hand, and holding the cream can with the other hand. I was in the backseat holding the egg crates down. There were eggs flying everywhere. We took the eggs to DeWald's grocery store, and told them to buy the good eggs and throw the rest. I grabbed the supplies we needed. We were in a hurry to get home for fear of getting caught in another blizzard.

At that time, Highway #34 was between the LeRoy Buck and Orville Ketterling farms. That road was a lake! We drove on top of water and ice, broke through the thin ice, and drove back on water. The old, green Model A did not give up, and we got back to our farm that day!

When we were in Streeter, we sold the cream to the Cream Station which was owned and operated by Calvin Villhauer. He was the younger brother of my grandmother, Christine Villhauer Dockter. It was a strange meeting. I had met Calvin way back in time when I was a child. He came to Grandmother Ritter's home while we were in Wishek visiting her. I think the reason I never forgot him was because he had a beautiful, little red-haired daughter. She had long, red braids, and was always walking close to her father. Her name was Peony. Grandmother told us that her mother had died, and she was always walking close to her father.

The month of May went down in history. We had snow, mud, and more mud. The fields were potholes and mud. I don't remember how we got the crop in. We lost calves to disease because of the wet, cold weather.

A great deal of wheat was being sown as late as the fourth of July. It was now or never, and some of it did yield well. We had a field of flax seed that did not mature to the ripe stage, and did not get harvested until the next spring.

Another plague that came with the muddy spring was mosquitoes in swarms. It was almost impossible to be out in the open for man or beast. We did not have any protection or spray!

The historic levels snow, rain, and water that year caused major flooding of roads and lowland areas. The lakes which formed at that time became permanent and still exist! Some of the roads never appeared again. State roads were built around the lakes!

14

FARMING

Electricity and Running Water

My parents did not recover from my announcement of getting married the week of my seventeenth birthday. Instead of a high school education, they gave me a dowry that consisted of four milk cows, two bred yearling heifers, a blonde wood bedroom set, a table and six kitchen chairs, and $150 for a Maytag kitchen stove. My mother gave me twenty chickens, a goose and gander, a duck and drake, canned goods, and a hog that we butchered when we did the family butchering for the year.

I appreciated everything they gave me. However, I think they gave me too many milk cows because it reached into their budget of what they needed.

Father's farm had electricity in 1948 when I got married. The farm Art and I lived on did not have electricity until 1958. Art's father, Matt, owned the land where we lived, and did not allow electric poles for a long time.

Father put an old, gas motor into Mother's old square-tub, Maytag washing machine. That washing machine was, maybe, older than I was. I was delighted to simply have a washing machine with a gas motor in it. Because they had electricity on their property, Mother also gave me her kerosene and gas lamps, and her gas iron.

The condition of the farm buildings where I lived was pathetic. It was indescribable. What I did not know at the time I got married, was that I would not have running water or a bathroom until I was thirty-one years old.

The Dugout, Cross Fencing

After Art and I purchased the farm and became engaged in farm and soil conservation practices, there were many projects in which we could participate. One of them was pasture rotation. This practice was designed to keep pasture grass from being overgrazed by the cows. Overgrazing destroyed the roots of grass, and made the pasture unproductive.

The program we chose was cross fencing by splitting the pasture acres into four pastures. However, the problem it created was "water." We would have to dig a well for each pasture. This created more problems. Each well had to have a gas motor pump, a windmill, or some form of power. The work and the problems were big.

I visited the County Agent's office often to discuss Homemakers and 4-H projects. I also looked at the new soil conservation programs. There was an article in the local Homestead paper about a dragline coming into Logan County. They would dig dugouts to conserve water for pasture cattle. This project would be the answer to our problems.

One day I was at Napoleon, and decided to go into the Agricultural Soil Conservation Services (ASCS) office. I signed up for a dugout.

In those days, women did not even go into an ASCS office. I informed my husband that I had signed up for the dugout. He said, "What if they do not find water? What will you do with a hole in our pasture?" What if? What if? What if?

This was a new project in Logan County. The people in charge of the project were not sure exactly when the dragline crew was coming. A surveyor came to our farm pasture to mark the area that had the most potential to produce a dugout with water.

One day, we were on our way to town. Behold, there was a huge hole in our pasture. It was the dugout, and there was no water in it. The dugout was about the size of a farmyard. There was a pile of dirt on each side the length of the dugout about ten feet high! It was humongous! My husband was furious! "What will the neighbors think? What will my father say?"

A member of ASCS came out to our farm to see the dugout. He was very positive about it. He said that we needed to wait, and see the spring snow runoff. We had high hopes that there would be water in the dugout by spring which was six months away.

Spring came after a hard winter of heavy snow. The dugout was not a subject that was brought up any longer. We were looking at pastures, and checking the condition of our fences. They break after the thaw of heavy snow that rests on the barbed wire. When we got close to the dugout, we were amazed to see that it was filled with clean, clear water. The slough and the little pothole in the pasture turned out to be a huge watering hole for the cattle to drink! It was our answer to one problem in farming. We signed up for another dugout. Eventually, we had a total of five.

Our next project was cross-fencing. This required several miles of new fencing. The fence would be put up with steel fence posts spaced approximately twelve to fifteen feet apart. After the posts were pounded into the ground, one barbed wire would be strung on the posts to set up a straight fence line. After the first wire was attached to the posts and stretched tight, two more barbed wires would be attached to make the fence into a three wire, barbed fence.

At the time, I was wearing a back brace, and there was not much physical work in me. In the month of June, there were some city boys who were looking for summer jobs. Jerry Schumacher had helped us with fieldwork at one time. He came to help with the fencing project. LaRue Jundt was another neighbor boy who helped with the project. They both had some experience with fence fixing, but they had never put up a new fence.

I said, "Jerry, you will be the post pounder, and LaRue will learn how to stretch barbed wire with the stretcher." They were excited about the project. It was a challenge for them. We used a wagon attached to a small tractor that had all the equipment, steel fence posts, and barbed wire they needed. I followed them with the pickup truck during the project to provide any other needs they had. These two boys and I put up several miles of strong, barbed wire fence.

LaRue Jundt became a Baptist minister later in life. I do not know what profession Jerry chose. I do know they were good, barbed wire fence builders.

Our family is currently leasing the pastures to tenants to provide grazing for their cattle. To my knowledge, the dugouts are still in use.

My Farm Business Contribution

My father-in-law, Matt Rudolph, was born in Ukraine. He came to America, and filed a homestead claim in North Dakota in 1906.

After Art and I purchased the farm (1,600 acres), there was a great deal of work and responsibility to manage. It was a big business at that time, and we should have hired full time help during the spring and summer season. The problem was no one would work for Art, he did not want to pay the wages. I did any kind of help, including going to town to get parts and supplies.

My in-laws, Matt and Sophie Rudolph, lived in Napoleon, North Dakota. This was the county seat in the town where we did all of our business. Sometimes, I stopped at their home to see how they were. At that time, Glenny was a toddler, and Grandfather enjoyed showing her toys and books.

One day, Matt asked me what Art was doing. I said he was working in the field. He said, "And you are driving around while he is working?" Sophie never drove a car. He went on to tell me that women should not have any part of the business. They should not even discuss business. "The only right they should have is to answer the husband if he asks them a question."

In 1962, the Farm Service Agency sent us a Wheat Acreage Allowance. We were told we could only seed an allowed acreage, and there was a penalty for excess acres of wheat. Our wheat acreage was a total of 200 acres.

After the fields were sowed, they had to be measured with a 16½-foot A-shaped acreage rod. Since our fields were irregular, they had to be measured at both ends. It was a lot of walking to measure the length and width of each field. It was a relief after the fields were done, and I took the measurements to the Soil Service Agency in Napoleon. After all this work — walking, measuring, and driving to the soil service agency — my father-in-law thought I was only "...driving around with the car."

I remember the day when the radio announced that steelworkers were on strike again. The decision was made by the steel company to close the steel factories, and move them overseas to other countries. Machinery parts would be manufactured overseas, and local farm equipment companies could basically not stock parts anymore. However, they could stock parts that were commonly wearing out.

We were farming with used machinery, and experienced many breakdowns. It was my job to go to the local equipment shop and get parts. I went home from the field, washed my face, and put on a chambray work shirt over my dirty jeans. Then I drove twenty miles to Napoleon, and stood in line with about thirty men who were also waiting to buy or order parts. When the crops were ripe and waiting to be harvested, standing in line and waiting for parts was not easy for anyone. Sometimes, the manager would call some of the neighboring towns in order to locate some parts. One day, I drove 200 miles to get a part! That was another day when "I was just driving around with the car."

Heavy Farm Equipment

There was plenty of hard work once we purchased and began to live on our farm. I plowed with a small tractor and a 2-plowshare in a field that had rocks. The rocks could detach the plow several times in one round. Each time, I had to keep the tractor running with a foot on the clutch, and do a backbend to attach the plow to the tractor again!

By this time, we were making hay for 200 Hereford cows, and we farmed with heavy equipment. We had 200 acres of alfalfa which I swathed twice in a season. The swather was a self-propelled, motorized machine which cut the crop, and put it in a row to be cured for hay. My daughter, Glenny, learned how to rake hay with a new hydraulic rake. She was a very good tractor and rake operator at age ten!

Another job I had was to swath the wheat. It needed to cure, so it would be ready for the combine to thresh it. Then it would be ready for storage.

When the time came for crop rotation, we planted 200 acres of corn. Since there were no herbicides for weed control, I cultivated the corn with a 2-row tractor and cultivator. The cultivating had to be done three times in a season. 200 acres times three is 600 acres covered.

When the corn was ready, we cut and stored it for silage and winter feed for the cows. I operated a large tractor that was hitched to an ensilage cutter machine. The same tractor that pulled the chopper, also pulled a trailer which contained the chopped corn. It took three persons to do this complex job. One operated the chopper and trailer. The second person drove loaded trailers to the farmyard, and the third person operated a tractor to pack the corn pile.

While all the above procedures took place, another project awaited me. We had about 200 acres in summer fallow. These fields were not planted. We had to till them to restore nitrogen in the soil, and keep them free of weeds. It took about three cultivations in a season to control the weeds.

While I was busy, my husband plowed, ran the grain combine, and repaired machinery and pasture fences.

Rock picking was an unending project. My first experience was when my brother was ten years old and I was eight. My father took LeRoy and me to a rock field. In those days, it was equal rights – women and girls had to do the same amount of work as men and boys. That day when we got to the field, Father said I should pick rocks about the size of a grapefruit. It was a horrible experience.

I don't know which was worse for a little girl – picking rocks or pulling corncobs off the corn stalks in the field. One Saturday morning when I was eight, Father took my brother and me to the corn field. It was windy and cold, and I did not have gloves. I wore my leather mittens, and could not get a grip on the corncobs. I was so cold, I started to cry. The tears froze on my cheeks.

My father said to me, "Sit on the wagon. You're not much good in the field." It was cold on the wagon too.

Back to the rock picking project. This work never stopped in my life until we quit farming. Removal of rocks took place in the spring after crops started to grow in the field. As soon as Art was done seeding a field, I started the rock picking project. Sometimes, there was a delay because of heavy rains.

I operated a tractor that had an automatic, front-end loader attached. There were hundreds of acres to cover. Two hired men picked up rocks, and loaded them on the front-end loader. After the scoop was filled, I drove to the rock pile and dumped the rocks on a pile. About the time we quit farming, most people were investing in rock picking equipment or hired rock removal.

Mystery Garden

In the North Dakota Soil Conservation Program, farmyard beautification began with planting a shelter belt of trees. The trees were planted eight rows in an "L" shape. The design was laid to protect the farmstead from the unending Northwest wind. The soil was prepared by resting the plot for one year to prepare a good, weed-free seedbed.

The day the soil conservation team came to plant the trees, we had a rain during the night. The planting went well; however, there was one low place that was too muddy to plant the trees. It was a low place that was close to the farmhouse, and also well sheltered from the Northwest wind.

Several weeks later, I was looking at the plot that was too muddy to plant, and I thought, "Why not?"

It was late in the planting season by then. I mixed all the seeds, and planted them by hand broadcast. I just threw the seeds everywhere, and used a garden rake to cover them.

I was working in the fields by then. I forgot about planting the garden. One day, I looked at the garden plot. To my amazement, all those seeds had germinated!

We did not have the summer rains as usual. There was something mysterious about this garden. The crops of fields were not good due to lack of rain, but the garden grew and grew. Almost anything grew – watermelon, muskmelon, etc. These are crops that do not do well in the North Dakota climate. We came to the conclusion there was a "spring" at the base of the garden plot!

Our family shared a great deal of vegetables with our neighbors. The muskmelon was a cross with the cantaloupe, and it was a heavy bearer. There was so much of it during the ripening season, I purchased 2-gallon buckets of ice cream. I split the muskmelons in half, and filled them with the delicious, frozen dessert. We had invited some friends to join a group of neighbors. The event turned out to be a corn and muskmelon picnic. Eventually, it was hosted by neighbors, and became an annual event. There were as many as fifty people at the outdoor picnic.

These are the events I miss. Most of the neighbor community has been dissolved due to senior retirement and younger people going into other business fields. What I miss about our farm is, "the mystery garden!"

The Shetland

The Edwin Rudolph family left the Rudolph homestead farm and moved to a farm in South Dakota. They had one daughter and four sons: Earl, Sheila, Darrell, Darcy and Cordell. They had a family of boys and also had a Shetland pony. The pony's name was Pal. They eventually outgrew the pony. Glenny was a few years younger than her Rudolph cousins, so she got her first pony.

Pal was quite old when she got him, and he also needed some grooming. He was a smart pony. We could see that Pal was trained to cut cattle when we were driving cattle from one pasture to the other. When there was a cow going the wrong way, Pal showed the cow the right way to go! He lived in the barnyard until everyone had outgrown him.

Our family used to invite Glenny's city cousins to the farm: Charmaine, Jolene, and Kelly. With Glenny, they were the four "pretty girls." They needed to do really novel things. They were too big to play

131

dolls, so they did mostly outdoor activities. They all took their turns riding Pal. There was also the stock tank. They used it to skinny-dip. They thought they had the privacy of the corral boards and did not have to deal with clothing. While they did not have their clothing on, they thought they could conveniently ride Pal in the nude. They knew that they were about two or three miles away from civilization.

Grandfather Julius was at our farm one day. He was busy repairing the outside of our chicken coop. He said the girls looked like they could paint the chicken coop. My plan was to cultivate field corn that afternoon. I set the girls up with old clothes, buckets of red paint, and paint brushes. Then I went out to the field to cultivate corn.

After about two hours, one of the girls came running out to the field and said, "Florence, you have to come home! The girls got into a paint fight and they painted Glenny's long, blonde hair red!" I went home and washed Glenny's hair. It was red oil paint. The shampoo removed the oil, but not the paint. So, they made a redhead out of a blonde!

15

FRIENDSHIP FORCE

The Good Old Days, Travel in the Late 60's, Central America

In the late 1960's, Eastern Airlines offered plane tickets for $500 which allowed a person to fly to any of the fifty states, plus thirteen foreign countries. These included Bermuda, Jamaica, Yucatán, plus all the Central American countries. Twenty-one days were allowed for travel. For each destination, the traveler had to fly into their hub at Atlanta, Georgia.

Art and I chose to buy the tickets, and spend three days each in Bermuda, Jamaica, Yucatán, and Guatemala! We each packed a 14 x 22 suitcase containing three changes of clothing, and carried them on the plane because we could not afford to lose our luggage.

We completed our trips to Bermuda, Jamaica, and Yucatán. Our culture shock was overwhelming.

Then we went on to Guatemala City. Guatemala was the jewel of our trip. Our hotel was huge, and was built by Pan American Airlines. They used beautiful, orange ceramic tile (the Pan-American colors), and added an impressive, open air restaurant and dining area.

We did not know that there was a military coup the day before we came. The streets were quiet, and there were a lot of soldiers with guns on their backs. We went on with business as usual. We did not have reservations for scheduled tours, so I approached the manager of the hotel for points of interest.

The manager hired a guide to take us into the jungle. This guide took us about forty miles in his car to a small park. It rained sheets, and crashes of lightning were everywhere. Ahead, was a metal bridge that looked aflame! He drove calmly, had his arm on the top of the seat, and was talking nonstop. He took us to a place that displayed the oldest civilization in South America, the Olmec civilization. In this park, we saw about nine statues of huge faces. They were approximately six feet tall, and carved out of stone. Each face had a perfect resemblance of the caps, headgear, and glasses worn by our astronauts when they went to the moon.

How were these discovered? In the late 1800's, a farmer was digging in the soil and found one of these large statues. Later, the remainder of the statue faces were also found and unearthed.

There were four civilizations in Mexico. The Aztec, the Maya, and the Inca are well-known, but there is little information available about the Olmec. I saw replicas of an Olmec face on a three-foot scale in Austria. I don't know if they were carved in stone.

When my grandson, Collin, was twelve years old, I asked him to look up "Olmec" on the internet. The description was not close to what we saw with our own eyes. Those figures were small with large heads and bright colors. I pointed out to my grandson that the figures on the internet did not resemble the real ones, but that my story was true. My grandson said, "Grandma, none of this may even exist, because they can put anything on the internet."

"Collin," I said, "I was there in Guatemala. I saw the faces, and they are real."

The Friendship Force

Rosalynn Carter was the official Chairperson of The Friendship Force International. The President and Mrs. Carter were guests of the President of Brazil in Rio de Janeiro for ten days, and developed a wonderful friendship. Rosalynn did not get much attention as First Lady. However, she believed that more people should be able to participate in an experience like they shared in the international exchange! She intended the Friendship Force to be operated on a volunteer basis.

The program material was sent to every governor in the United States. Each governor was to appoint a director to contact people in their state inviting them to sign up for travel to foreign countries. Initially, the destinations were unspecified. There were many people who could apply.

The object of the program was to promote peace and friendship with other countries. She wanted to help Americans understand other cultures, and to create an exchange so people from other countries would have an opportunity to understand more about America.

My sister, Inez, lived in Minneapolis, Minnesota, and read about the program in her city paper. Of the hundreds of people who applied, she and her daughter, Charmaine, were accepted. They had never been overseas. My sister kept me informed as her program moved along.

She told me that each state governor had the material. So, I wrote to my governor, Arthur Link. He said he was unable to draft a volunteer coordinator. Two weeks later, he wrote again and said that he had successfully appointed a coordinator and the program would begin. Sadly, within two weeks that coordinator died, so a replacement had to be found. When the governor was able to appoint a new person, he informed Art and I that we would be accepted as participants! By now, the rules were changed, and we were told which city would participate in the exchange. It was Hamburg, Germany. Our daughter, Glenny, also came with us and lived with a German girl, Christina.

Eighty Americans were chosen and flown to Germany. Shortly after we arrived, we watched eighty Friendship Force Hamburg residents eagerly board that same plane to be guests in homes in Bismarck, North Dakota! The exchange was for seven days.

We were hosted by foreign families who were oriented to the project like we were. We were taught to accept any lifestyle, any customs, and any standards of living — if they were proper.

We were hosted by a thirty-seven-year old plumber who lived with his seventy-year old mother. The program was not new to him. He had been in previous exchanges between Hamburg and Spain.

These were the most interesting seven days of my life! Our host's name was Herbert. He spoke English and during the first days he interpreted for his mother. Fortunately, our language barrier did not last long because we spoke low German (Schwebisch), and some high German sayings and church hymns that I remembered came to life.

Herbert had the week planned and we had a wonderful time! We attended a Mozart concert, and went to the Rembrandt Museum to see Leonardo di Vince's original fifteenth century drawings. We saw a fish market at the Hamburg seaport, and went dancing on a ship. We saw many other sights and attended remarkable events. Herbert returned the visit one year later.

We were excited when we were notified that Herbert was coming to North Dakota to visit our farm! He was supposed to arrive at harvest time, and we were seriously wondering where we should take him — possibly to the Four Faces of Presidents in South Dakota or the Yellowstone Park? Since it was August and the crops were ripe, we could not take long vacations. When Herbert arrived, we discussed the plans and choices we were considering.

Herbert said, "I do not want to go anywhere — I want to see your farm. I like it here. I want to help you work on your farm." He drove tractors, trucks, and tried pitching hay with a pitchfork! It was a very good Friendship Force exchange we had with Herbert.

Christine also came to America to visit Glenny. They communicate closely to the present time.

In 1982, Art and I participated in a no-hosted exchange with Russia.

When Japan hosted an international youth exchange program, we were privileged to have a high school student live with us for three months. The next year, we traveled to Japan and were offered hospitality by her family. What a wonderful sharing there was! At this time, we also traveled to China and South Korea for no-hosted exchanges, and were privileged to tour Hong Kong.

The next year, we took part in hosted exchanges with Egypt and Greece.

"Since its founding in 1977, the Friendship Force has brought together millions of people. Today [there] are ... more than sixty countries, promoting friendship and goodwill through an extensive program of home hosting, or exchanges. [The] founding day was March 1st, 1977, World Friendship Day."[1]

Friendship Force in Russia 1981-82

Our second experience was a no-host tour into Russia. The tour was coordinated by a brilliant, young Jewish attorney from Minneapolis, Minnesota. This took place before the Iron Curtain came down.

My husband, Art, and I were the only participants from North Dakota. There were eighty passengers. Many of them were Jewish who were in search of long displaced relatives. Their goal was to find some of them on this unusual trip to Russia. However, after making entry through Finland and arriving in Russia, the rules of that country came down. We were not to even try to visit any residents, to take pictures of anyone, or to use any recording devices.

All our stays were in Russia at the Intourist Hotel. As tourists, we were fortunate to get tickets to go to the Bolshoi and the Leningrad theaters. The average Russian citizen did not have the luxury of theaters.

A number of meetings were scheduled for us which usually included detailed studies of problems their country was experiencing. Most of the presentations were not interesting and seemed to go nowhere.

One day, however, I had a most interesting experience as we attended a luncheon hosted by government staff. There were long, narrow tables and I had the opportunity to be seated across the table from the Secretary of Agriculture! Art and I were the only farmers in our exchange group. They understood we were farmers because Art wore cowboy boots.

---

[1] https://www.thefriendshipforce.org//who-we-are/ Friendship Force International, Our Story, August 8, 2019.

To my right, there was a young businessman from Minneapolis named Dave. He hoped to learn many things about this huge country. Dave said to me, "When this man is done speaking, ask a lot of questions."

I said, "What should I ask?"

"Ask him anything that comes to your mind. I will back you up. This might be the only chance we have."

After the secretary, Mr. Natya, completed his presentation, the meeting was opened for questions. I queried, "Mr. Natya, you stated that you had enough animals and that more production will solve your problems. My question is, how do you propose to do this and when?"

He answered, "By doing more research and providing better strains of grain – as you do in your country. This will take time to do."

"Why do you have a shortage of meat animals?"

"Because our country has a cold climate and we cannot make enough hay for the animals. Also, we don't have enough grain for them."

"My husband and I have 1,600 acres of land and we make enough hay for 150 cows."

Mr. Natya said, "Our weather is much colder."

Dave cut in and said, "This lady lives in North Dakota which is on the same latitude as Moscow." By this time, the Russian officials had their calculators on the table and were breaking acres down into the Russian hectares. They said it was not possible to have that acreage in their country.

I answered, "Sometimes extra help is needed."

Mr. Natya said, "It is illegal to hire help in our country."

This was my chance to help him understand. "In my country, we have free enterprise. When calving comes in the spring, we take turns sleeping so we can keep track of cows calving. Some nights we don't sleep at all. Every calf we save is money in our business. The harder and longer we work, the better chance we have of making our business work."

I asked a further question. "You stated that you did not have enough milk and dairy products. How are you going to solve this?"

"We are going to breed and raise dairy cows the way your country does. Like the black and white ones – the ones that have the big (gesture with his hand) to milk."

I helped him out, "You mean the udder?" The crowd soared with laughter. It became a fiasco, and everyone seemed to enjoy it. All these terms were new to our city friends.

Mr. Natya had a soft smile come over his face and said, "I was in your country. I saw your potato fields in Idaho, your dairy cows in Wisconsin, and your corn fields in Iowa." It was obvious he liked what he saw. He continued, "We find that by allowing each family one hectare of land, they can produce enough potatoes for the entire population."

"Why don't you let them have two hectares?" There was more laughter.

"Because they cannot have anyone help them."

Now, this went right back to free enterprise. This was the part of our discussion with which they could not agree. It was an enlightening session enjoyed by all. There was no formal planning. We just simply looked at the whole picture.

Soon, it was time to return. When we got to the airport, there was a long line at the check-in which did not seem to move. We saw clothes all over the counter. It was a search. We were petrified.

The Russians knew exactly where we had been and what each one of us had done. From those who had visited homes, they confiscated cameras, film, tape recorders, pictures, and all forms of communication. When it was our turn, however, they just pushed us through. They never opened our suitcases.

They separated our coordinator, Steve, from his wife and our group and held us up at the airport for two hours. After the negotiation, we were reunited, and the officials assured us that we were all able to leave.

It was a sad departure. For some people this was a sad time, because they feared the relatives they had visited may have been placed in jeopardy. The Jewish people had good intentions by visiting Jews. However, they broke the Russian rules. The Russian government cut relations for the Friendship Force for two years. It was sad for the Friendship Force.

It was a good experience for our group. It renewed our appreciation for the freedoms we take for granted in America!

Friendship Force – Finland, Russia – Original Notes

Friendship Force to Russia
Two days orientation in Helsinki, Finland.

Finnish people are friendly. Helsinki is very clean – with all goods and things we have.

Taxes are high – income taxes range from 35% to 80%. People who own homes are considered wealthy. Owning land is referred to as a "fortune".

We flew to Moscow. The contrast is very obvious. First thing that night, we went to see Red Square. We also watched the changing of the guard at night at Lenin's tomb.

We had a Friendship meeting at Moscow's Friendship House. We met with instructors from the University of Moscow. They spoke excellent English.

We got tickets to the world-famous Bolshoi theater two nights at $3.00.

First night–opera, "Barber of Seville"

Second night–ballet, "Wooden Soldier"

The average Russian citizen never gets a ticket to Bolshoi – only tourists.

Tour of underground Metro system. It is one of the best in the world. Very few cars.

A tour of USSR national exhibit.

Went to a nursery school by group.

We were free to go on group tours or on our own.

There was a shortage of consumer goods.

We went to Leningrad by train at night. A Pullman. 11:30 PM to 7:30 AM.

Toured Leningrad. Visited Pisharevskae(?) Cemetery where 1½ million people are buried in mass graves. This was from the 1,000-day siege when the Germans surrounded and starved the city of Leningrad.

We attended church at a Russian Orthodox Church. One of four churches in Leningrad. Mostly elderly widows and tourists who attended.

We went to see Catherine the Great's winter palace in Leningrad. Now is Hermitage Museum.

Ballet of Leningrad. "Creation of the world," Andre Petra.

We drove out to the country twenty-five miles to the summer palace of Paul I, son of Catherine the Great.

We visited a child's outpatient center.

No one owns land. Everyone lives in apartments, except farmers.

Will share with civic groups.

Highlight of tour – meeting with Secretary of Agriculture.

Friendship Force – Egypt

Art and I participated in a Friendship Force exchange with Egypt. Of all of my world travels with Friendship Force, Egypt stands out. In a few days, all of this happened to us.

We were met by our host at the airport in Cairo. His name was Albi Wahlia, a tall, dark handsome young man. He was in a business partnership with his cousin, Ahmed and his wife, Allma.

Our flight came into Cairo early in the morning. Egypt was in turmoil. Their president, Anwar Sadat, had been assassinated! The vice-president, Hosni Mubarak, had been sworn in just hours before we arrived. Our hosts were instructed to bring us to the town hall to meet him. When we arrived, President Mubarak shook hands with us, and greeted us as Friendship Force Ambassadors from the United States.

Our Egyptian host, Albi, took us to El Alamein, the World War II battlefield, to see hundreds of abandoned tanks. It was General Rommel's last stand. He was defeated fighting while he was on his way to the oilfields of the Middle East which Hitler wanted because he was out of fuel. We saw hundreds of monuments to soldiers of all nationalities that were killed in that horrible, historic battle.

Albi took us on a cruise of the Nile River. It began where the Mediterranean Sea touches the Red Sea. Many years ago, when the Pharaoh freed the children of Israel from slavery, this is where Moses took them through the Red Sea. The people began their long journey to the promised land – now called Israel.

141

My grandfather, Gottlieb Dockter Jr., used to read the German Bible to us. He mentioned the Egyptians and the children of Israel frequently. He spoke high German and Russian. He did not learn to speak English. In German, he referred to the Egyptians as "Yeagibsa." I wonder what he would say if I could tell him that I went to Egypt, and saw where Moses and the Hebrew people crossed the Red Sea after the Pharaoh released them from bondage!

Back to the cruise on the Nile. The Red River in the United States and the Nile River are the only rivers which flow to the north. Giza and the pyramids were an "outstanding site." Luxor is known for its obelisks and other monuments.

The Abu Simbel Temples monument portrays the Pharaoh Ramses II and his court. It had been there thousands of years and was located in a lowland valley near the Nile.

Egypt was planning to build the Aswan dam near this area. Many foreign countries were also interested in supporting this important venture. In order to get the necessary location for the dam, engineers in charge of the project had to dismantle the Abu Simbel Temples monument, move the pieces out onto the banks, and reassemble it. It now stands there as beautiful as ever! The engineers then were able to complete the building of the world-famous, Aswan dam.

After traveling in forty foreign countries, Egypt was the most interesting! I enjoyed the pyramids, the monuments of the pharaohs and queens. History was engraved in stone that goes back thousands of years. I also admired the engineering skills of the Egyptians. They taught the use of water from the Nile River which gave life to Egypt.

16

DIVORCE

Cooking In My Teenage Marriage/Silent Treatment

The first year we were married, I had a lot to learn about keeping supplies on hand. When I left home, we had a basement, electricity, a refrigerator, a cistern, and I only lived two miles from town. The house I lived in after our marriage did not have a basement, electricity, or a refrigerator. There was no way of preserving food, and we lived twenty miles from town. We had plenty of mice in the house too!

It was spring, and Art was working in the field. I was milking ten cows, and feeding the stock cows and other farm animals. The canned food my mother had given us was used, and there was not much of anything to prepare. I decided to make knoephla soup, one of the labor-intensive dough dishes. The only ingredients I needed for the broth were flour, eggs, cream and milk. I also had a can of Spam to serve with the soup. When my husband came home for lunch, he saw the knoephla soup. He put his cap on, and went back out to the field. I took some lunch out to the field at 4:00. He refused to stop and eat. He ate dinner that night, but never talked to me for a week.

I noticed he did not talk to me when things were not working with chores or animals. I was getting the silent treatment. This time it was a personal attack on me. Needless to say, I never cooked the great German Russia food in my household.

That was the beginning of the silent treatment that I got for thirty-three years. It was for any reason. I may have laughed at the wrong time, said something, or done something. He always had a reason to go "into the box" for one week – two weeks. This went on for years. As time went on I found out that his mother had the same nature.

Eventually, I lost my ability to laugh and cry. I never had anyone to share anything with. I was lonely in my marriage.

It was a shame that I carried around and covered up for many years after the divorce. I could not admit it to myself.

Dear Grandma, My Marriage Came to an End

Dear Grandma Katie,

Red flags. Before Art was drafted into the Army during World War II, there was a lot of talk between he and his family about a girl he was dating. Her name was Annie. Six months after he joined the military, he received a Dear John letter from her. She informed him that she had gotten married to a military officer, and was pregnant. After Art was discharged from the service, he carried a picture of Annie in his billfold with his personal ID.

After Art and I married, I saw the picture of Annie in his billfold. Her name came up often, and I always had a negative remark about her. After ten years, her picture was still in his billfold. Every time I commented negatively, he said, "You are jealous."

I told him, "I'm not jealous. I'm stuck with you, and I'm angry."

I had two nervous breakdowns. The last breakdown I had, I reasoned with myself that I did not love him. I chose to live in a loveless marriage for the sake of two beautiful daughters. After both of our daughters finished college and were married, I chose to end my marriage. The last seven years, we were not on speaking terms.

I endured forty years of loneliness, lovelessness, and no communication. I had covered up the mental cruelty and silence that lasted for days, and sometimes weeks. I had learned how to cover up for my husband, as my mother had covered for my father's addiction. (Our relatives and the community were aware of my parents' situation.)

When I told my mother that I was divorcing Art, she was outraged and disgusted. She did not have any sympathy for me. She told me I was crazy. She liked Art very much because he worked hard, and was not an alcoholic. He was closer to her in age, than he was to me.

My mother shamed me and felt sorry for herself. She said that my sister, Inez, had multiple marriages and divorces, and now I was divorcing my husband too! She said I was making her look bad. "How do you think I feel?" she asked.

My mother spread the gossip of my divorce to aunts, uncles, cousins, neighbors, community – anyone that would listen.

The divorce relieved me of the stresses and abuses I experienced in my marriage. It was a relief just to be alone and away from that environment. However, it brought other losses into my life, losses that could not be avoided or seen.

There is no winner in a divorce. I lost half of my friends; they took sides because they did not know what the problem was. I lost half of my family because they took sides. I lost half of my home and half of my lifetime earnings.

Three years after the divorce, I met and married a man, Elder Scherbenske.

17

GOODBYE ELDER

Goodbye, Elder Scherbenske

Goodbye Elder Scherbenske,
Goodbye to the excitement you felt about meeting me, and our first dinner date.

Goodbye to the first marriage proposal you made when you told me how much you loved me – a feeling I did not have at the time. Your response was, "I will chase you until you catch me." And you did.

Goodbye to the many times you asked me to marry you. Your motto was, "I want to marry you and take care of you."

My response was, "I don't need a caretaker. I just want someone like you to love and to have that love returned, as you are doing." But I also reminded you that a three-month courtship was too soon to get married.

Goodbye to the day when you bought the engagement ring. We were both so excited. I was reluctant to wear it because your children were so hostile when you told them that you were in love.

Goodbye to the time when you carried the engagement ring in your pocket, and told all your friends, "She is going to marry me on May 23rd."

Goodbye to a beautiful courtship. You were kind, loving, caring, considerate, a gentleman, companion, and confidant. You carried me on a pedestal, and it was the most wonderful eight months of my life! Life was beautiful for both of us. We had plans to spend a free and leisurely retired time: golfing, relaxing, traveling, and enjoying each other. We were compatible in so many ways. We could spend hours together talking, and never running out of things to say. Or we could just sit and look at each other, and do nothing. And so, we were married.

Then, just a week after we were married, there was a reminder that you had an appointment at Fargo Clinic with a urologist. It turned out to be a biopsy. Three days after that, there was a call from Dr. Toni. The report was a malignant tumor of the bladder. How could this be? How could our lives go from the happiness we knew, to such a horrible stage? This was not in our plan.

When we could calm ourselves down to where we could begin to reason, we talked it over with the doctor, and decided to go to Mayo Clinic. We were in for more shock and horror when the doctors told us that treatment was removal of the bladder, and a complete exploratory of the internal organs. Prior to that, there would be a week of tests to determine if your body was healthy enough to survive the surgery.

The eight-hour surgery took place, and went well! But there was one thing that did not go as planned. The two surgeons were looking for me in the waiting room, and the look on their faces was like steel. They told me the surgery was a success. They removed the bladder, and made a neo-bladder out of eight inches of the small intestine. This would be completely functional, but the cancer was an aggressive cell that was already in the lymph node system. You had to undergo chemotherapy. My first question was, "What are his chances with the chemo?"

The answer was, "Thirty percent."

Goodbye to the eleven days you spent recovering in the hospital. Your three children still had not acknowledged your cancer. Your son had called the nurses' station twice for your condition, but did not speak to you. Your pain was so terrible, and you were allergic to all narcotic pain killers.

It was then that the doctors counseled with me every day. They built my strength, so I might be able to support you — and be strong enough to go through the journey of your recovery, and the chemo that was to follow.

It was then that my anger grew for your children because they left me alone with their father when you needed them most. It was then that you told me how you bailed them out of two or three divorces each, and nursed their invalid mother for fifteen years. Now that you needed them, not one of them was there for you.

But our love continued to grow. Goodbye to the time when you asked me over and over, "Would you have married me, had we known?"

I said, "Yes." You told me I would not be sorry, and I am not.

Goodbye to your prayers when you thanked God every day for bringing us together. Goodbye to the love and praise you showed me.

Goodbye to the tenth day of chemo, when your full, curly head of hair fell out, and how depressed you were. You could not understand how I could love you. Our love was being expressed more and more every day. By then, you did not smile anymore. We cried a lot. You hurt so much, and pleaded that I should lay my hand lightly on your arm so you could relax and go to sleep.

Goodbye to the last chemo treatment after six months, and within two months your curly mob of hair grew in again. We continued our journey, and lived one day at a time. We never spoke about the chances of the cancer returning.

We went ahead with the Mediterranean cruise you had planned and canceled for our honeymoon. It was June, and you were at your best again! You had a childlike radiance and happiness, and enjoyed every minute of it. The cruise was the best thing we did in the two years of life because you were so happy.

Goodbye to the early fall in August. Your daughters slowly came around, but your son still was not speaking to you. You seemed to have more tired days than energetic days.

I was in denial. We went to Mayo in September, and the CT scans and all tests came out clear. But why the tiredness? Later we went to Fargo for tests. They were clear too. In October, the tiring was constant.

The first week of November, we went back to Mayo for more tests. This time, the liver did not test quite normal. Back to Fargo. Tests for two days. No change. By now, it was obvious that you had lost all energy, and could barely stand up to walk. I was still in denial, as I had always been. We went to the hospital in Fargo on November 23. On December 2, 1994, your suffering came to an end.

Goodbye to the kindness you showed me. Goodbye to the self-worth you taught me. Goodbye to the prayers when you thanked God every day for sending me to you.

Goodbye to the fight you put up for life, and your steadfast faith that our meeting was not in vain – that it was God's plan, and that our meeting will continue in heaven. Goodbye to every time you opened a door for me when I went somewhere – when you stood at our garage door, and held it open when I came home. And I know that when the gates of heaven open for me, you will be there. Goodbye to the two years that you needed me most.

P.S. The day I checked Elder into Mayo Clinic, there was a Persian rug on the waiting room floor. The Shah of Iran was there with his entire court. He was in the last stages of cancer, and was there for treatments. He died. Cancer is a respecter of none.

Thank You, Elder Scherbenske

During Elder's recovery from the surgery, his children were not visiting him. There was no communication. After the chemo and radiation treatment, there was also the threat of cancer recurring. Elder decided to will his house to me to assure me that I would have a place to live if he died.

I lived in this house six years after he passed away. Though it was a beautiful, three-bedroom house in a new neighborhood, I was not happy living there after he was gone.

He went to work when he was fifteen, got married when he was seventeen, and worked hard all his life. His two older brothers went to college.

I felt that Elder was so generous and concerned about my welfare, I decided to do something in his honor. I gifted his home which he gave me to the University of Jamestown, North Dakota. This provided an endowment for an annual scholarship in Christian education.

Goodbye, Elder Scherbenske.

Closure: Overcoming Childhood Stress

It took a lot of healing and strength to recover from the stressful life that I came through. I was fortunate to find the "Beginning Experience" support group. It taught me to live my life, and not make the same mistakes again. It taught me that though I cannot change others, I can change myself. I found out some things about myself that I did not like. I had to change myself.

Dear God,

I thank you for giving me the insight and desire to come to this serene place to heal myself from whatever your will so desires. I am grateful that I may heal myself of all the hurt and pain that I have experienced in my lifetime and especially the last seven years.

Teach me the way I might learn to love myself first that I may learn how to love others. Teach me to trust myself so that I may trust others. Teach me to forgive myself so I might forgive others. Fill me with goodness so that I may reach out to others.

Beginning Experience

"Beginning Experience" is a support group that offers a healing experience for any loss in life, i.e. the loss of a loved one, or the breaking or ending of a relationship. They use Bryce Fisher's "27 Building Blocks."

18

CLIMBING THE MOUNTAIN

Climbing the Mountain, Self-Encounter

After my divorce of a marriage of many years, I prepared to climb the mountain to get to know myself. Before packing for the climb, I had to clean out my backpack. The more I took out of the bag, the more there seemed to be in the bag. When I got to the bottom of the bag, I couldn't believe how far the issues reached into my childhood — and beyond that, even to the time before I was born. I had to put all the pieces of my life together before I could start climbing the mountain. I could not rationalize the strange feelings and experiences from my childhood and later in life. I was there, but no one ever saw me.

My parents were both Germans from Russia descent. My mother was seventeen and my father was twenty when they met. At the time my parents were dating, my paternal grandmother was dying of cancer. Her wish was to see my parents get married. The family arranged to have my parents vow that they would love, honor, and obey each other until death at the foot of my grandmother's deathbed. This was a fulfilling wish for my grandmother; however, it was not a joyful beginning for my parents' marriage.

Their first child was a girl and they named her Florence Pearl. When Florence Pearl was one year old, she was diagnosed with Wilhms' disease, a cancerous tumor on the kidney. She

died at the age of twenty months. Two months after her death, my brother, LeRoy, was born. When he was almost two and a half years old, I was born. They named me Florence Helen. My mother said I was a disappointment because my appearance was so different from the other two children. I also reminded her of my father's younger sister whom she did not like.

My father was an alcoholic before he married. His drinking started in Grandfather's wine cellar. My mother was an angry person. As we grew older, we found out that my mother had been molested by her stepfather when she was thirteen. This possibly explained some of her anger. Her anger did not stop there. It reached down to my older brother which manifested itself in his temper tantrums.

As I got to digging deeper into my backpack, I found more evidence and realized that I was the sibling next to my brother. My father's addiction and my brother's temper often created open combat on a battle-ground. My brother took all his frustrations out on me because I was a target on the rung a step below him. The abuse was there as far back as I can remember. It is just now while I'm still trying to clean out my bag to get ready to climb the mountain that I can identify the different forms of abuse he put me through. It was every form of abuse imagin-able. I'm beginning to realize that the feelings I had about myself since my childhood were real.

When our family came to completion, I had four younger siblings. My mother spent most of her time working outside helping in the fields. She also worked close by my father and brother so she could step in between when the feuding began between the two. I believe there could have been male envy between my father and LeRoy because LeRoy got more attention from our mother. They were both vying for nurture and attention. My mother never punished her son for any kind of behavior. LeRoy got some brutal punishment from Father.

I cannot remember ever playing with dolls, toys, or games. As far back as I can remember, I was doing something for my younger siblings.

It seemed I could never do anything well enough. No matter what I did, I could not get my mother's approval.

I kept digging deeper into my knapsack. I found that by the time I was ten years old, I had complete charge of the household and was responsible for four younger siblings! I can hear the words ring in my ears today: "Watch the kids so they won't get run over on the highway," and "Keep them away from the stock tank so they won't drown." It was my duty to prepare the noon meal (butcher a chicken if there was no meat), get the vegetables from the garden, and get lunch ready to take to the field.

The deeper I got into my backpack, the more incidents there were of the criticism by my mother. She would compare me with an aunt who had a big nose, and a step aunt who was of incorrigible behavior. My mother was still passing on shame.

There was a reminder of the migraine headaches I had since I was six years old which became longer and more frequent. My mother and my aunts would discuss my migraine headaches and they all agreed that it would get better after I started to menstruate. They would whisper the word, "menstruate", because I was not supposed to know what it meant.

One day, I overheard Father and Mother in heated conversation talking about my headaches. My father said, "If that crazy son of yours would stop pounding her head, it would get better."

Mother's reply was, "You and your crazy ideas."

By now, I'm beginning to realize I will never get this bag cleaned out to go mountain climbing. There is no end to this. I'm about fourteen by now, and the flashbacks have not stopped. The boys were starting to notice me. Some of them told me I was pretty. How can that be because my mother always said my hair was not nice, my teeth were too big, and my nose was too large? Many times, I was annoyed when the boys complimented me because I didn't know what to say. I firmly believed that I could not be anything but homely because my mother said so. My brother also confirmed it and reminded me of it repeatedly.

I started dating when I was young and the boys who dated me were young. God took good care of me. I was lucky not to get in a serious relationship until I was sixteen when I met a man thirteen years my senior.

I got married to him the week of my seventeenth birthday. What I did not know at the time of my marriage was that my husband was not any more mature at the age of thirty than I was at seventeen.

I can't believe still more stuff is coming out of my backpack! I see here that my husband's personality was exactly like my mother's! How can this be since they never knew each other? He is just like her. He never approves of anything I do. He always criticizes me, and never tells me he loves me or compliments me! I don't remember telling him I loved him either. Maybe he was just a vessel to get out of that dysfunctional family. Could it be? My marriage came to an end.

Well, what I see here now in the backpack is that I have spent years healing myself of all these issues that were discussed. The main issues were denial, fear, anger, guilt, and shame. Of the five mentioned, shame was the greatest.

I can go before a group now without guilt and shame and say that my father was an alcoholic. He was a sick man and went to his grave not knowing of his illness.

And so, where do I go from here? Where can I put the blame? On my mother who deprived me of my childhood and has since died of Alzheimer's? My brother who would deny his actions? My marriage is over. So, who is left but me?

I chose to leave home at age seventeen to marry an immature man who was much older than I. Did I marry to escape a miserable home life?

Does it help to put blame on anyone? No. I have to pick myself up and make the best of what I have left in life.

19

4-H Related Activities, Jocie, Glenny

My Cousin, Mildred Dockter, and 4-H

My Uncle Edwin and Aunt Elizabeth had five daughters. I did not get to talk or play with them – I only saw them in church. They came to the little church on the hill ¼ mile from our farm. The church was on a 160-acre tract of land which my father inherited from Grandfather Dockter.

We went to church every Sunday. My father always walked to church early in the winter mornings, and built a fire in the coal stove. The church was warm in time for the service. There was one hour of Sunday School and one hour of worship sermon. This was a two-hour service, and was a long time for children. We did not understand the service because it was in high German taken out of the Bible.

I can still remember how I was gazing at my cousins: Mildred, Thelma, Eleanor, Loretta, and Priscilla. Their mother, Elizabeth, was artistic and sewed identical dresses for her five girls. The fabric was taffeta, and the skirts were three-tiered with lace insets. They had dresses in colors like yellow, pink, light blue, and always the same patterns. They looked like five dolls.

In the summertime, I talked my parents into allowing me to walk to my cousins' farm. It was about two miles down a gravel road which was a long way on a hot day. I was nine years old, and my sister, Inez, was five. She insisted on going with me, but she was lean and lanky and could not keep up with me. She always got her way with crying, so I had to pull her all the way. We were allowed to stay two hours which proved to be a hard and tiring afternoon for me.

Our parents did not communicate much with Uncle Edwin and Aunt Elizabeth. Eventually, they were not communicating at all. It was then that we lost touch with our cousins until later in life — after we got married and we were busy with our families.

In 1998, my older brother, LeRoy, did a search on the Dockter lineage that went back to 1615. He came up with 2,400 descendants! He compiled a book listing all the relatives and how they were related to each other. At the same time, there was a family reunion in Bismarck, North Dakota. There were approximately 300 people listed in his book that attended this reunion.

It was about that time, my cousin, Mildred Dockter Thurn, reunited our cousin relationship. She talked about childhood times, and reminisced about our Grandfather Dockter Jr. and his kindness. She told about the time when Mrs. Gideon Breitling organized a 4-H club. My sister, Inez, and I were invited to join, but our parents did not allow it. Mildred and her sisters told Grandfather about the subjects that 4-H offered. He thought it was a very good program if it taught girls to cook, sew, and keep house. Grandfather Dockter offered to come to the Edwin Dockter farm, pick up the girls, and bring them to the 4-H meeting in Venturia once a month. He brought them home to the farm after the meeting. It gave them a chance to interact with other families and cultures.

4-H became popular in rural areas and small towns. It took the place of home economics which was not offered at that time in schools. I remember how hurt I was when my cousins joined 4-H. I was not able to do any activities outside the home.

After I was married and my husband and I had established farming, I was invited to join a local Homemakers Club. Later, I became a 4-H leader, and both of my daughters became 4-H members. There were many good projects.

I began sewing my clothes when I was ten years old, and also made my own patterns. After I was a 4-H leader, I learned how to lay a store-bought pattern correctly. It was much easier to sew clothes after using patterns.

In 4-H, I learned a great deal about public speaking. It was my favorite subject. It was a good experience to start "Demonstration and Public Speaking" early in life. Some of my 4-H girls thanked me later in life for introducing the subject to them when they were young.

Bonnie and Betty Flemmer

Art and I got married in 1948. I was new in the community. Jocie was born in 1952. The Flemmer family came to visit us and to see the baby. In those days, it was customary to bring food that was easy to prepare. They brought a box of groceries that contain snacks, canned fruits and vegetables, and a noodle soup mix. They had a son who was two years old, and Betty and Bonnie who were about eight and ten years old. My baby was six weeks old. She did not sleep much. She had colic and I was holding her that evening most of the time.

The Flemmer family moved out of the community about the time Betty and Bonnie went to college.

There was a church ½ mile west of our farm. Many years later, I saw a notice in the local newspaper of a funeral service for Sarah Flemmer. I went to the funeral at that church and was happy to meet Bonnie and Betty and their families. Their father, Herbert, had passed away. Sarah, their mother, had been a 4-H leader in the community.

Bonnie and Betty invited me to a family gathering after the funeral. While we were at the gathering, we reminisced about the night their family visited our house when Jocie was a baby. They said, "You were such a young mother and you had this pretty baby. And you breast-fed the baby. Then you went into the kitchen and fixed a 'light lunch.'"

They described the dishes I used. They were cream-colored China with gold, tiny flowers and trim. They were a wedding gift from the Schnabel hardware store. We received another service for six, cream-colored China with gold wheat sheaves and trim from the Weidman hardware store in Venturia. These were generous, beautiful gifts from both hardware stores. Bonnie and Betty were impressed with the dishes.

They said, "We wanted to be like you. When we were playing, we each wanted to be Florence. We took turns being like you."

Tangerine, Wool Suit

The spring catalog, Alden's, came every year. This catalog had a cover model with a light blue, two-piece suit. It was trimmed in white braid and had a front zipper. The skirt had three kick pleats front and back. I spent several days gazing at it — wishing I could have it, but the price was $29.98. That was more than our weekly household budget in those days. I thought about sewing it. It was a difficult design jacket. It had wide, mock shoulder panels that extended beyond the set-in sleeve and was on the fabric that extended into the princess style bodice.

My mother knew about my fantasies, dreams, daring, and risks that I had experienced many times. I talked her into buying wool fabric, 62 inches wide, a soft tangerine color, at $2.98 a yard. I needed two yards. At that time, I had not laid a pattern yet. I drew the pattern on newspaper for the princess jacket and pleated skirt. The jacket was lined. The fabric, zipper, and braid trim were a total cost $7.50. There is not a picture of me wearing it. However, there is a picture of my sister, Inez, wearing it. When I showed a picture of the suit I designed, my friends would say, "Your sister is beautiful!"

By this time, I had designed and sewn most of my clothes including a burgundy topper as that style was described, and a pink wide wale corduroy coat that I wore over my wedding dress because it was cold outside. I had never used a commercial pattern. After I was married, I made my own patterns, but I also used some purchased patterns.

Jocie's Wedding Dress 1973

When my daughter, Jocelyn, was nine, I became a 4-H leader. The major 4-H projects were Nutrition, Home Management, and Clothing. It was in one of the clothing projects I learned how to lay a purchased pattern correctly. I was obsessed with the tailoring project. 4-H girls completed their projects at age nineteen.

My daughter went to college and later got married. Getting ready for her wedding, we went to several shops looking for a wedding dress. Using our knowledge and sewing skills, we decided we could save a lot of money by sewing the wedding dress. It took me back to the days of making my own patterns. However, there were now more options because I could use many patterns on that one dress

While she was trying on dresses, I noticed she liked a bishop sleeve (a set-in sleeve to the elbow which then balloons down to a slim wrist), a bodice of lace with covered buttons from the collar to the waist, and a shirred skirt that came to a bustle back with a five-foot train. The skirt and train had a double layer of sheer, polyester organza.

Our next step was to go to Mrs. Bowles Fabric Shop! I needed three patterns to get the style she wanted. Some of them came from my pattern box. There were approximately 40 yards of fabric in the dress, including the veil of silk tulle. There were scraps of lace left from the bodice to make the head dress for the veil.

The cost of the fabric was $70. The dress style she chose was marked $695! The pricing for these purchases took place in 1973. It was exciting to see the project as it was put together! For me, it was an extension of my childhood experience to make something out of nothing and to get what I want.

Jocie – Area Woman of Fargo

I am excited about an article in the magazine, "Area Women of Fargo." My daughter, Jocie, was on the front page in December 2005. The interview was about her job as CEO of the Renewable Energy Coalition Council of North Dakota. This involved renewable energy of corn, soybeans, wind, and coal. The project was in its infancy stages with a lot of potential. I am very proud of her achievements.

In the article, she tells about her growing up in a small farm community, playing outdoors, and riding her horse. She did not mention the time she spent with the dogs. She was an only child until she was eight.

I did a lot of work in the fields at the time. However, I always felt there was not the potential for physical work in her because most of the time I couldn't find her. She was hiding somewhere with a book! It was the book — the love of her life from toddler to this day. She graduated with a bachelor's degree in home economics, a master's degree in dietetics, and later a master's degree in communications.

She has two adult daughters, Sara and Jenna, and she is an ovarian cancer survivor. She is in partnership with her husband, Virgil Iszler, in a farm operation.

P.S. Jocie received the 4-H Achievement Award of North Dakota at age nineteen and was named an Ambassador of 4-H. In 1971, she represented North Dakota at the National 4-H Convention in Washington DC.

Glenny's Employer's Christmas Letter To Me, 2018

Hello Florence,

I hope this Holiday greeting finds you well and enjoying the Season. You and I have met a few times, but you may not remember me. I am a good friend of your daughter, Glenny.

For me, 2018 has been a year of reflection. I have had many struggles over the past thirty years and also many celebrations and joyous times. One thing that remains constant is that Glenny has always been there for me and a part of my life whether things were going great or whether they were not.

We met over thirty years ago at work. We were both competitive and strong women, so you can probably imagine we weren't instant friends. As far as work goes, she has always given it her all — and that's a lot. She has undeniable work ethic and dedication. That is evident in the success she's achieved professionally. She really gave me a run for my money and eventually surpassed anything I could hope to achieve. Her focus on excellence is transparent in everything she does.

Our friendship took time and truly getting to know each other at our best and our worst. Glenny has seen both sides of me, and what is remarkable is that her love for me has remained constant. She is a true Christian — the truest I've ever had the privilege of knowing. It is not something I will ever take for granted.

Twelve years ago, I lost my husband. I tell you this only because it was at that time that Glenny met my brother, Jim. They had the opportunity to talk and get to know each other during the funeral and visitation events occurring at that time. Although it was only an hour or two, Glenny had a profound impact on my brother. He unknowingly, at that time, was terminally ill and focused only on my healing and grief. He came to me at the end of his stay and told me what a remarkable person Glenny was, and that surely God had put her in my life for a reason.

He told me, "She is someone you need to keep close in your life. She's in your life for that reason." He passed away a few short weeks later, and reminded me to keep her close. I will never let her go.

I think I have been compelled to send you this Holiday note to make sure I thank you for giving the world such a wonderful person and example. And she is an example of conviction, integrity, loyalty, and love. The world is a better place because of her. I wanted you to know.........

With love,
Corinne

Glenny's Adventures

When Glenny graduated from high school, she applied for a summer job in Medora, North Dakota. This little town is on the western border of North Dakota and Montana. It is known as an area where Teddy Roosevelt was engaged in ranching and producing beef cattle. He was always fascinated with cattle and other animals. President Roosevelt was known for his support of national parks throughout the United States.

161

Medora was located on US Highway 10. After the drought and financial crash of the 1930s, there was only a bar and perhaps a mail service left. The governor of North Dakota became interested in rebuilding Medora to its original state. Now there is a musical play which portrays Teddy Roosevelt's life that runs every night from Memorial Day to Labor Day in September.

In the spring, parents would get letters from an administrator describing available jobs. Glenny's application was accepted. One of the suggestions was good walking shoes. We shopped and bought Rockport shoes with a cork sole. Glenny was assigned table waiting at an ice cream shop and assisting in a kitchen with any work that came along. She enjoyed her job and came home with $1,300 in her pocket. That was a lot of money in the 70s! Her shoes were worn out. The soles were good on the outside, but her toes dug holes on the inside. That was a lot of walking!

Glenny had another adventure. After her second year in college, her friend, Kathy, called her to come to Texas and join a harvesting company. The manager of the company, Mr. Beitz and his wife, called Glenny and offered her airfare. She was to help harvest, run a combine, and drive a semi grain truck to the grain terminal in Oklahoma. The plan was to start harvest in Texas and harvest all the way up to North Dakota. It was the tractor driving experience she had in her childhood that qualified her for that job.

I believe these job experiences convinced her to finish college — and that she did. She graduated from college with a bachelor's and master's degree in business. This took place after one of her high school teachers told her that she was not "college material." I am proud of Glenny!

Glenny married Jeff Carter, a teacher, and they have two sons, Bryce and Colin.

20

RECOVERING FROM SHAME

Closure – Shame

My mother told me so many times all the things that were wrong with me. My hair was too thin to make braids. When my two front teeth came in at age six, she said they looked like shovels. My nose was getting larger all the time. She said I would become an old maid and compared me with an old maid in our community.

My mother, Helen, passed away at age eighty-five. I could not forget the many times she corrected me in conversation with relatives and friends. I also remembered she did the same to our father.

After she died, I was so upset because I could not grieve her. She was my mother, no matter what! I went to a counselor. After she had the information about my family and my life, she asked me about my mother's life. My mother was ten years old when her father died of flu in 1918. When she was thirteen, she was molested by her stepfather. This left her a great deal of shame.

The counselor said, "Your mother never recovered from that shame. She passed shame on to you, her oldest daughter, and that was you, Florence." It also robbed me of my self-esteem. It was another thing added to my unhappy childhood.

The Receiver of Shame

Reasoning: I never did anything of which I had to be ashamed. Only my mother and husband criticized my nose. I consulted with a cosmetic surgeon. He told me that my nose was the best feature in my face because its size was the best and it was in the right place on my face.

My mother had a French provincial vanity with a three-way mirror. When I was a child, I used to put curlers in my hair, and I could see the back of my hair in the three-dimensional mirror. I could also see my nose. I always worried about my nose. What could I do about it? When was it going to grow? When would it stop growing?

My mother was sewing a dress for me when I was about eight years old. While she was fitting the dress, she told me I was "hippy." That was another subject I had to worry about when I was a child.

21

LEE

Lee

My second cousins, Georgie Hopkins and Barbara Fanta, lived in Jamestown, North Dakota, where I retired. They were active in the senior citizens club. When they invited me to join them at the Vets Club for dinner, I found them seated at a long table for twelve. They were all widows from the senior center, except Georgie. He was the only man. I was introduced to all the ladies. There was one empty seat where I was not to be seated because it was reserved for someone who was coming.

Later, a man came in and sat in the reserved seat. Cousin Georgie introduced him to me. His name was Lee.

Several weeks later, I was dancing with someone at the Vets Club when the music stopped. Lee was standing in front of me, and we broke out in laughter. He was dancing with his daughter-in-law, Nancy, and I said, "Oh, you do dance?"

He said, "No, no. I can't dance."

The next week, my cousins, Georgie and Barbara, were at the club again. We walked in the door and Nancy saw us. She said, "Lee is here. You should dance with him. Ask him to dance. He is too bashful to ask you."

After the dance that night, Lee asked me to go to coffee. We had a quiet place in the restaurant. Lee was a quiet, introverted person and was listening to me talk. Every time I stopped talking, he would say, "Don't stop talking." He was looking at my face and watching my lips. The first time we met, we knew that we were attracted to each other.

We had several dancing dates, and he said, "I want to learn to dance because I want to dance the way you dance." That night he took me home, walked me to the door, and asked, "May I kiss you?" I knew then that we were in love.

We were both sixty-five and Lee still worked part-time. There was no plan to get married. We did not live together. He was a 4:30 riser. I got up later and moved slowly in the morning. But we did spend every evening together. I would invite him to my house for dinner or he would take me out dining somewhere.

We would go dancing often wherever we could find dancing music. Sometimes, we drove 100 miles to go dancing. We both enjoyed classic, modern, country-western, and gospel music. Every time we went to a performance or concert, Lee would purchase a disk of the program. He gave the discs to me, and I had shelves full of them. We never had time to play some of them.

Lee was a kind, handsome man and everyone liked him. There was something about his personality that attracted people to him. I was fortunate to be able to be in a relationship with him for eleven years. He said, "I will go anywhere you want to go because I want to be with you."

Lee was not wealthy. However, he shared everything he had with others. He was shopping for jewelry for me often and surprising me with gifts I. I told him I had more jewelry than I could wear. He gave me cards for my birthday, Mother's Day, Christmas, and Valentine's Day. His slogan was, "You have my heart." Roses came with the cards. He was always expressing his love for me. Every day was special. Just being with him was a joy to love him!

Lee and I enjoyed traveling throughout the United States. The highlight of our travels was the Danube River cruise. The tour started with three days in Prague, Czechoslovakia. The fourth day, we embarked at Nuremberg, Germany, and cruised to Vienna, Austria. Then we cruised down the Danube River. We had port calls at Bratislava, Slovakia; Budapest, Hungary; Croatia; Belgrade, Serbia; Spitsov, Bulgaria; and Romania. The cruise ended at the Black Sea, and we flew back to the United States.

Lee had a heart attack at age fifty. He was a very active, hard-working person, and made regular visits to his cardiologist. He died of a heart attack at age seventy-five. This was a tragic loss in my life. He has been gone a long time, and I still miss him.

22

HEALTH FAILURE

Health Failure 2016

March 20, 2016

During the winters of 2014, 2015, and 2016, I lived as a snowbird in a mobile home park in Mesa, Arizona. I experienced bronchitis at that time. My daughter, Glenny, said I should have a thorough lung examination after having bronchitis three years in a row. In the spring, she made an appointment at a heart and lung clinic. The doctor at the lung clinic did a complete, two-hour examination and diagnosed my lung function as very good.

I also had an appointment with a cardiologist. I have had high blood pressure for a long time. The heart doctor seemed to be more interested in the blood circulation veins in my legs. His diagnosis was that I needed surgery on these veins which would open up the valves in my leg veins. He suggested changing my blood pressure medicine. He also prescribed heavy-duty elastic stockings because this medication for blood pressure would cause swelling. I needed to wear these elastic stockings six months before my surgery so Medicare would pay for the vein surgery. I started taking the medicine and wearing the stockings the latter part of March (2016) and I had an appointment for vein surgery the first week in December.

In May, six weeks after I started the medicine, my sister, Inez, and I were at a family gathering. We were driving to my home, she noticed that I started to slur my words. I suggested we go to an emergency room. We drove to the nearest one where they did a CT scan. It showed a TIA stroke. I had some distorted vision and it affected my speech and taste, but there appeared to be no physical handicap. I could still have a normal life.

When I came home, my doctor changed my medicine, because the stroke was caused by high blood pressure. He also referred me to the hospital for observation. There were three doctors waiting for me. They did tests, scans, and an MRI for three days and did not find any more brain damage from the stroke. The doctors prescribed the medicines they were giving me. After the three days they had me in the hospital, whatever they were doing to me made me sick.

After they discharged me, my legs were stiff, my ankles and feet felt like leather, and I could barely walk to the parking lot to meet my daughter. The next day was even worse. My head and neck ached. After a few days, I noticed the medicine I was taking was a statin to "lower cholesterol." I was allergic to statins! I stopped the heavy dose of statin, but my symptoms were the same. I was aching all over my body. I had never been so sick and achy miserable in my life. I could not sleep, I lost my appetite, and I was depressed and horrified. It was the beginning of my body's breakdown.

I was living in a three-bedroom condominium in North Dakota. It was then that my daughters, Glenny and Jocie, decided I must move out and move to Arizona where Glenny and her family lived. I was too ill take care of myself.

My initial experience at Nunnencamp assisted living in Friendship Village was the worst experience of my life. My home was a studio which was beside five electric transformers. My nerves were needling me. My muscles were cramping. It was hell and I prayed and wished to die every day!

I became sensitive to electricity, anything magnetic, the wireless telephone, television, the microwave oven, the transformers (anything with electricity), the power of the Internet, iPad, anything that was made from oil, polyester, nylon (all synthetic materials).

My body reacted to all petroleum products, plastics, and synthetics. I had muscle cramps and nerve needling. I wanted to die, that's all. I could not wait until I could take a sleeping pill and go to sleep in the hope that I would not wake up. I always thought God was not listening to my prayers.

My daughters went to great lengths to help me through those horrible days. I moved within the assisted living to a small apartment and created an all-natural environment. They got rid of my polyester clothes and bedding and searched to replace them with fabrics that my body could tolerate. My clothes and bedding are now made of cotton, wool, rayon, and silk. I have all-natural leather shoes with leather linings. My one-bedroom apartment has a lovely, wool carpet.

While my body went through all these attacks, I became weaker all the time. I lost my sense of taste and, as a result, also lost a lot of weight. I was still wishing every day that I could die. A friend of mine (from the same resort where I lived in the past), came to visit me after he heard about my health problems. Cal was shocked when he saw my condition. He came and took me for a ride several times a week or just came to visit me a couple times a week. He always encouraged me that I would get better.

Getting Back Into Society

My body was weak and recovered at a very slow rate. Doctors could not diagnose my condition. I had suffered a physical and nervous breakdown.

Now, I am careful not to expose my body to powerful magnetics and lights. I don't go to movies, and limit the hours of television to which I expose myself.

My body is sensitive to all petroleum products. There are very few products which do not have a petroleum base. Synthetics are made of petroleum and include plastic, detergents, most cleaning products, cosmetics, and many fabrics.

I react poorly to all synthetic fabrics such as polyester, nylon, Dacron, and acrylics. Many of them have a percentage of natural fiber and a percentage of synthetic. These blended fabrics are not only used in clothing, but also in mattresses, bedding, and floor coverings. It is difficult to find natural fabrics.

A key to my recovery has been to surround my body with natural fibers such as cotton, linen, wool, silk, rayon, cork, rubber, and leather. I wear all cotton and natural fiber clothing, and my leather shoes have a leather lining. I sleep on a cotton mattress, sit on a cotton fabric sofa, and my chairs are leather.

After I lived in a synthetic free environment as much as I possibly could, I believe my body breakdown was caused by stress. I did learn that God is in charge of my life because He did not let me die when I wanted to die. He was not done with me!

My recovery was so slow that I did not realize I was improving. I am getting to enjoy life again. The tremors of my body and hands have improved a great deal. I am able to write again. I enjoy my friends, go to live theater, and keep in touch with my family.

23

PERSONAL DEVELOPMENT
AND ACCOMPLISHMENTS

Florence Dockter Scherbenske–Personal Development–
Resume 1987

Public Contact and Leadership Management

1958 – 1982	Sunday School Teacher
1962 – 1982	Volunteer Leader, 4-H
1965 – 1966	President, Local Homemakers' Club
1977 – 1978	
1987 – 1988	
1967 – 1968	President, Logan County Homemakers' Council
1978 – 1979	
1968 – 1973	Member, Church Board of Administration
1970 – 1972	Secretary, Logan County Planning Commission
1975 – 1976	President, PTA
1979	Member, Streeter Jubilee Committee
1979 – 1980	President, American Legion Auxiliary
1984	Chairperson, Jamestown Centennial Quilt Committee

1984 – 1986	Hostess, Jamestown Fine Arts Association
1984 – 1986	Scholarship Chairperson, North Dakota Homemakers' Extension Council
1984 – 1986	Vice-President, Church Women United
1985	Conducted 30 Passenger North Dakota Homemakers' Extension Council Tour to Colorado, Estes Park
1986 – 1987	Secretary/Treasurer, Jamestown Apartment Association

Education

American High School, Chicago, Illinois.

4-H Leadership Training Classes, North Dakota State University. 12 hours per year. 1962 – 1982.

Adult Education Classes, North Dakota State University – Family Life, Home Management, Foods and Nutrition, and Clothing. 4 hours per year. 1960 – 1987.

Travel Career Institute; Extensive study of international and domestic travel and tourism, American Airline SABRE Computer System Study. 1987

Arthur Frommer Seminar, 1987.

Travel Experience

United States–44 states including Western region, Eastern and New England states, Southeast, Central, and Alaska and Hawaii

1969	Central America–Yucatan and Guatemala
1969	Canada, Bermuda and Jamaica
1970	Central America – Mexico
1973	Europe–England, Netherlands, Germany, Italy, Austria, Switzerland and France

1982   Asia–Russia and Finland
1984   Orient–China, Hong Kong, South Korea and Japan
1985   Middle East–Egypt and Greece
1994   Mediterranean–Crimea, Ukraine, Turkey
2003   Norway
2004   Canadian Rockies
2005   Eastern Europe
2007   Australia

Other countries I have had the privilege to tour include:
Bulgaria, Croatia, Czechoslovakia, Hungary, Romania, Serbia, Slavia,
Israel, Scotland, New Zealand, and the Fiji Islands.

Professional Public Speaking

4-H Leadership Public Speaking, 1962 – 1982.

Dale Carnegie Course 1983

Showed travel logs of twenty foreign countries to community and civic
groups. Developed and presented demonstration, "How To Pack a
Suitcase with Minimum Amount of Clothes. 1983- 1987.

Honors

Twenty year 4-H Leadership Award

Closure - My Accomplishments In Life, Self-Education, Personal Development

My Quest For Knowledge Has Never Ended

My mother told me I could not learn because I could not read and memorize the Heidelberg catechism. This was printed in high German. At
home, my family spoke a lower caliber dialect called Schwebich German.

In the short time I was allowed to attend school, I learned to read English. It was a gift of God. No one could stop me from educating myself! They could also not stop me from using the opportunities that were out there in the world of business and all other fields of life!

I read the Reader's Digest for thirty years and kept all my copies for reference. National Geographic's was another favorite of mine. I was not interested in fiction of any kind.

Graduation from American High School, Chicago Illinois

As a young person, I was never allowed to attend any classes in high school. I was an adult when I had the desire to graduate from high school. I wanted to get all the knowledge that I was deprived of when I was a child. I was on my own now. I could make my own decisions.

The first subject required was "How to Write an Essay." On the subjects that I took, the American School tested mostly by essay. After I studied a chapter, I had to express myself: what the solution was, what I thought, and why I believed what I did. I wrote hundreds of essays and believe that is where I learned my writing skills.

There were four required subjects: English, math, science, and social studies. After these were completed, I chose the electives which would be most useful and beneficial in my lifetime.

General Business helped me throughout my life. I became interested in studying consumer education and quality of products, bookkeeping and finances.

Public Speaking was the beginning of my leadership in 4-H and community activities.

United States and World Geography taught about the world and the location of countries. United States and World History explained when many events occurred. These studies awakened my desire for world knowledge and travel. It was the beginning of my world travels.

Another course was Home Management. I had a great deal of experience in that field. I had complete responsibility of the home in which I grew up when I was ten years of age! All I had to do was make some corrections and adjustments to fit the culture.

How to Dress Correctly. I learned how to use colors that are best for one's hair and eyes, which patterns are best for people who are short-waisted or long-waisted, which figures look best in long dresses or skirts, and what to wear when going to a business meeting or a birthday party.

Room Arrangement and Floor Plans. The bedroom: don't put the bed where you can see who is in it when you open the door. The living room: form a group of chairs and sofa in the center of the room to form a conversation area. Don't put a chair in each corner and create a long-distance conversation.

Etiquette. This was a good subject. It could benefit all walks of life. I wove some of the interesting, beneficial habits and points into our 4-H program. The group enjoyed some interesting lessons and had fun in our discussions.

Beginning Art proved to be an unending subject in my life. My interests ranged from animals to still life. Later, I appreciated visiting museums in America and abroad: Rembrandt, Leonardo da Vinci, the Sistine Chapel, and many others.

Physics. The structure of motors, RPM, and maintenance of equipment. These subjects helped me in my occupation with farming.

Also, Management of Housing. My husband and I owned sixteen low income apartments. I did the cleaning, painting, and leasing. We were still engaged in farming at the time.

24

LEADERSHIP AND
ACCOMPLISHMENTS

Rosebud Mission Program

The Methodist church has missions all over the world. I was a member of First Methodist Church of Jamestown, North Dakota. One of our mission programs for the year was usually a request for children's coats for the Indian reservation in Rosebud County, South Dakota. Our Methodist women's group had a dozen or two coats for the drive each year. The Rosebud Reservation requested children's coats because the children could not get a ride on the school bus if they did not have a coat. Children with no coat missed a day of school and the hot lunch they would have received at school.

I thought there must be another way to help these children so they could attend school. One year later, the United Methodist Women reported that the reservation would accept used coats. My first thought was of coats at rummage sales. After going to rummage sales, however, I found the search proved to be very labor intensive.

One day, I wandered into the Salvation Army Thrift Shop. After visiting with some clerks, I told them about the children's coat project

I had in mind for the reservations. They said their coats are put on display in the shop and after five weeks, they are removed and go to a baler for salvage. Salvation Army asked $1.00 for salvage coats, and they had fifteen coats available which I purchased. Some of the coats were soiled and had to be washed. It was a start, but was rather slow.

After this, Captain Tim of the Salvation Army showed some interest in the project. He said it was a wonderful project. He would offer full support of the program in any possible way including giving salvage clothes for Indian children.

The Salvation Army did not have the time or financial support for a project such as this. Captain Tim suggested that projects like the coat project were beneficial to the Salvation Army because people offer volunteer services. He proposed a meeting with a representative of our church and a reporter from the Jamestown Sun. The Jamestown Sun showed a great deal of interest and did several news releases on the project.

It was then that our committee was invited to inspect all the coats that were not sold on display. We went to the thrift store once a week and usually came up with fifteen or twenty usable coats. When we consulted with the Rosebud Reservation, they said they would take any size children's and adult's clothing, shoes, bedding and linens, etc.

We removed the seats of our twelve-passenger church van and shipped several loads of coats (approximately 2,000 coats)! After that, we sent loads of miscellaneous items. The last loads were blankets and bedding. I felt the bedding was the most rewarding. We layered the bedding flat on the van floor and stacked it to the ceiling of the van. It was a comfort to know that someone somewhere had the comfort of sleeping in a warm bed with a blanket from our church.

Our church sent a total of eleven van loads to Rosebud Reservation! The round trip was approximately 700 miles. The church provided the van and I provided the gas. We had volunteers that drove the van. Many members spent many hours preparing the articles that were sent to the reservation. There was full support from Pastor Pederson!

Rosebud Mission was very grateful for all the items they received, and it was a rewarding experience for everyone that took part in the project.

The Hoarder

The city I lived in had a population of 16,000 people. I knew the manager of the Salvation Army quite well. They were always short of money and supplies. I used to watch for sales at the grocery store, purchase food by the case, and would then deliver it to them. Eventually, the manager of the grocery knew what I was doing, and would notify me of the date of the sales.

I had a storeroom in my garage. It was a perfect place for a hoarder to store perishable food for the Salvation Army when they needed it. Those were the days when tuna would be on sale for $0.37 a can, and green beans were five cans for a dollar. There were many other good prices for food. I believe these donations were appreciated.

Quilt Making / My Quilt Collection

In 1984, I was appointed as chairperson for the Jamestown, North Dakota, Centennial Quilt Committee. After meeting several times, we discovered there were not many quilts in our community. The quilts people did have were family heirlooms and were very old.

During this time, many cities were celebrating Centennial events. The North Dakota State University Home Economics Department became interested in the art of quilting and offered courses. Quilting became popular throughout the United States, and hand-quilting became a craze.

Quilts were a luxury for those who had time and could afford the fabric. Quilting was also therapeutic. Women would have a quilting party because it was a source of entertainment. They did not have telephones or television. They also did not have many outings, especially in the winter months.

I had a large collection of quilts. The first quilt that got my attention was a yo-yo quilt which was shown at a moving sale. It had 1,600 yo-yos and sold for forty dollars. A yo-yo was made out of a round piece of fabric about the size of the top of a water glass. This round piece of fabric was stitched around the outside. Then the stitched thread was pulled tight to the center to form a puffed flower. This quilt was very old and fragile. My mother spent a great deal of time repairing the yo-yos. This quilt is still in our family. Glenny has it.

In those days, there were Ladies' Aid groups in many churches. These retired women enjoyed the companionship of other women in the church. Their purpose and goals were to accomplish projects which would benefit the church. Many of these women were good quilters with a great deal of experience. They charged $50 to hand-quilt a quilt.

I enjoyed designing and making quilt tops. At one time, I had a collection of fifty quilts. Many of those had tops that I designed. Others were patterns of old quilt designs like the wedding ring, grandma's garden flowers, the star, and the fan. One quilt had 200 hand-quilted roses. Hand-quilted quilts are rare and are a premium today.

I gave most of my quilts to my daughters, nieces, and sisters. I also donated quilts to organizations for fundraising. They sold tickets. The harder they worked, the more money they made. One organization made $1000 on one quilt!

Munsingwear Fabric

I used to go to Minneapolis by train and visit my sister, Inez, who lived in the cities at that time. She worked downtown and she knew her way around traveling by bus. We enjoyed shopping at the Munsingwear fabric factory. At that time, Munsingwear was one of the leading manufacturing companies for lingerie. There were also patterns available to sew lingerie. We would get up early, take a bus, and go to the factory to stand in line at 4:30 in the morning to buy nylon Trico fabric. The fabric was 102 inches wide and cost one dollar a yard. With two yards, you could sew a whole wardrobe of lingerie.

My husband and I were still living on the farm. The basement was made with poor cement and was a crumbling mess. My plan was to buy fifty yards of nylon Trico and cover the basement walls with it.

My parents were retired and living in Bismarck, North Dakota. My father came to our farm during haying season to help us make hay. One day, the temperature was 100° above with a windy storm. At lunch that noon, I said, "No one should be out there in that hot storm."

I thought Father might be interested in my project, so I asked him to come down to our cool basement. I had purchased rebar and hooks for the curtain rods, and had all the supplies I needed to cover our cement walls with nylon Trico. Father stood and looked at my plan. He was amused and wondered what I was going to do next.

He said, "This will be an easy project." While he was planning to cover the walls, he said jokingly, "Do you want to cover the ceiling too?"

I said, "I have fifty yards of white for the walls, and also have enough red for the ceiling."

He said, "It won't be hard to do the ceiling." Together, we accomplished the project. To use an old phrase – we made "...a silk purse out of a sow's ear."

The next day was 80° above, and we all went out to make hay in the field.

Art and I decided to quit farming and moved to Jamestown, North Dakota. When we left the house, I took all the window hangings and nylon wallcovering and put them in storage.

Later, I lived in a house that had a sixty-foot, paneled room in the basement. Some of my friends and I planned to cover the unfinished ceiling with the white nylon I had saved. We stretched twine across the 2 x 12 beams and attached it every three feet. Then, we looped the fabric loosely in the twine and the fabric covered the whole ceiling. It was the large room in the basement with the vintage ceiling that made the house salable when it was sold.

25

CLOSURE

Closure–My Mother's Hard Life

When they married, my mother, Helen Esch, was seventeen and my father, Julius, was twenty. She lived in a community of friends and many relatives in the Dockter family. However, she was a long distance from her family of siblings, mother, cousins, aunts, uncles, and grandparents. She was lonely in her marriage and community. The only communication was by mail, and she had to deal with the addiction of our father whom she lived with fifty years.

Mother lived a hard life: the loss of her father when she was ten years old and the abuse by her stepfather at age thirteen. After that, she was taken out of her mother's family and lived in her grandparents' home. She did not have much parenting or the parenting she should have had. She also lost two toddlers under the age of three to Wilms Tumor kidney cancer (Florence Pearl and Stanley Julius). After my parents were married, their first child was stillborn.

Did my mother know what she did to me? Did she know that I never had a childhood? Did she know I never had a doll, not even a rag doll? She told her friends I did not like dolls. She did not know how the assault in her early teen years affected her and her children. She did not know she was passing shame on to me or why she was doing it.

My Parents Provided and Cared For Us

My parents, Helen and Julius Dockter, provided and cared for me and my siblings the best they could. Our mother took good care of us when we were sick. I can still see her walk with the lamp when one of us siblings was crying with an earache. She put us to bed when we had a temperature, and we had to stay there until we were well. She bought fruit for us to eat when we weren't feeling well, even though there was not much available at that time.

She was upset when we were playing in the wet snow and came into the house with wet clothes. She said, "You are going to get pneumonia." That disease was always a threat before penicillin.

Rise Above Many Obstacles

I proved to myself that I could rise above:

being second to my brother,
being told I could not learn,
missing days in grade school,
having no high school education,
being deprived of my childhood,
losing my self-esteem,
being told I was a homely child,
being told my nose was too large,
being told no one would want me,
the shame I lived with.

Resume:
What I have done and where I have been!
You can do it too!

Preface or Closure

My days of denial were over. I conquered shame because it was not my shame to begin with. There was also guilt surrounding me and robbing me of wellness, peace and happiness. I became a whole person.

26

IN A NUTSHELL

In A Nutshell

Florence Dockter Scherbenske
McIntosh County, North Dakota
7/24/2005
Bismarck, North Dakota
Americorps Story
Registered in Library of Congress

This is a summary of a personal interview of Florence Dockter Scherbenske, and is registered in the Library of Congress. It took place in Bismarck, North Dakota, and the narrator was Lee Frey.

What memories do you have of your ancestors?

My ancestors were German from Russia. I vaguely remember my maternal great-grandmother. I was six when she died. She was born in Ukraine and was a midwife in Ukraine and on the prairies of North Dakota. She delivered over 1000 babies.

My paternal grandfather was a successful farmer in North Dakota, and acquired large tracts of land in the early 1920s. He gave each of his six sons a tract of 320 acres with the horses and equipment to farm that land. He gave each of his three oldest daughters 160 acres of land, six milk cows, and a complete line of household furniture. He compensated his two youngest daughters with homes and money. It was a great help to my sibling family because it provided a home and a living for us when the depression hit in 1929. We were poor, but not as poor as others.

Tell us about your childhood.

I went to a country school and walked most of the time or went with horses. Sometimes, I went by car. It was a one-room school. There were thirty children in all eight grades with one teacher. All learned how to read and were prepared for high school.

I learned to milk a cow at age seven. I could butcher a chicken and prepare dinner for a family of seven at age ten. At the same time, I was also taking care of four younger siblings while my mother worked in the field. It was a lot of responsibility to keep them away from the stock tank so they wouldn't drown, and to keep them off the road so they wouldn't get run over. My weekly allowance was five or ten cents.

Tell us more about your life.

I was born on a farm in a two-room house. When I married Art Rudolph, a farmer, we purchased a 1600-acre farm with an FHA loan. We raised small grains and had about 200 beef cows. Land was cheap. **These were the days of opportunity and hard work.** We had two girls and no boys. I was the right arm and hired man, and helped with all the farming and fieldwork. We seldom had hired help. The farm is still in the family.

We received the Logan County Soil Conservation Award. Ten years later, we received the North Dakota Agricultural Award. These awards were based on good farming practices and leadership.

What was the community like?

It was a rural community in a neighborly setting. Everybody had to pitch in to make it go. Most of the parents were involved. I took part in Band Mothers, PTA, and fundraising for cheerleaders' uniforms. I was a 4-H leader for twenty years. I taught Sunday school for twenty-five years, and was active with the Youth Fellowship. I was a leader in Homemakers Extension. The projects included Food, Clothing, and Home Management. It is a good program.

Did you have any hobbies?
I am interested in art. I saw many foreign art exhibits, and took some art courses. I enjoyed ballroom dancing. I made and designed quilts and had a collection of fifty quilts. I gave most of them away. I enjoyed gardening and flowers. I made arrangements and gave them away. I still garden, but no peas.

I enjoyed sewing. My mother taught me to sew without patterns because we did not have them available. I learned to design my own clothes, and sewed my clothes at age ten. I sewed two tailored coats at age seventeen without patterns.

You were a world traveler. How did you get started?
I toured forty foreign countries and all fifty states in America.

1) Land sales promotion. Flight to Florida.

2) Eastern Airlines. Canada, Bermuda, Jamaica, Yucatan and Guatemala City (Olmec, oldest civilization).

3) Mexico. Mexico City – first culture shock. Great surprise to see the archaeological discoveries of the pyramids in Mexico (late 1800's). Our trip was by car.

4) Seven countries in Europe: England, Netherlands, Germany, Italy, Austria, Switzerland and France. 1973. $1,500. for two. Fifteen days.

5) Friendship Force preparation. Rosalyn Carter – First Lady was Honorary Chairman. Bill Mushek. Ambassadors: selection, orientation (to accept conditions as they are), acceptance, the exchange.

6) Friendship Force exchange: Hamburg, Germany and Bismarck, North Dakota. (Hosted.) Our hosts were a thirty-two-year-old plumber and his seventy-two-year-old mother. They planned a full week of activities: Mozart concert and Leonardo Da Vinci's original, fifteenth century drawings in the Rembrandt Museum.

7) Friendship Force exchange: Russia and Finland. (No host.) We were hosted by university professors. Town Hall meetings were narrated by the Soviet Secretary of State, Soviet Secretary of Environmental Concerns, and the Soviet Secretary of Agriculture.

8) Friendship Force exchange: Orient – China, Hong Kong, South Korea, and Japan. (No host.) We had a visit with the Tucumsi family in Japan.

9) Egypt and Greece. El Alamein was a significant battlefield in North Africa during World War II. German General Rommel's defeat.

10) Mediterranean cruise: Turkey, Crimea, Ukraine. We had port calls at Constanza, Romania; Odessa, Ukraine; the Black Sea; and Istanbul, Turkey (Blue Mosque). (Trip with Elder.)

11) England. Point of interest – Stonehenge. Tour of London and Edinburgh. We were fortunate to get into the Tower of London to see the Crown Jewels. (Trip with Gladys and Don.)

12) Israel, Holy Land. Our tour covered the period of the Old Testament, the birth of Christ, and the history of His followers. (Trip with Inez, Gladys and Don.)

13) Norway. There were beautiful fjords, mountains, and waterfalls. Cities: Brendon and Oslo. (I took my granddaughter, Jenna Iszler, to Norway for her high school graduation.)

14) Danube River Cruise. Lee Frey and I toured three days in Prague, Czechoslovakia. Embarked at Nuremburg, Germany. Cruised to Vienna,

Austria. We had port calls at Bratislava, Slovakia; Budapest, Hungary; Croatia; Belgrade, Serbia; Spitsov, Bulgaria; and Romania. Took grand-daughter Sara to Australia and New Zealand.

(Note: My maternal grandfather was from Romania and died in 1918.

What have you learned in life?
I have learned to survive. I was a child of the dust storms and the Great Depression. Life was difficult, but we learned to live with little or nothing.

I learned to respect my ancestors for the courage they had to come to America. They laid the groundwork for us that we could have a better life. They were in search of freedom. The freedom that they found in this country. The freedom we take for granted.

What are you most proud of?
I am proud to be an American and to have spiritual freedom. I am proud of my two daughters. They are both college-educated, career women. I am also proud of my 4-H leadership, and the world traveling I experienced.

Do you have any regrets?
I regret the college education that I never finished. I wish that I had better parenting skills. I regret the time I missed with my grandchildren.

How would you like to be remembered?
I would like to be remembered as a person that lived an adventurous life. I had many good things happen to me – some were not so good. I have recovered from my troubled childhood.

I would like to be remembered as a **caring, sharing, and giving person** as I learned when I took hospice training. I feel I have received more in life than most have. God has been good to me.